UKRA Teaching of Reading Monographs
The advisory editor to the series is
John E. Merritt, Professor of Educational Studies,
The Open University, Milton Keynes

Already published
MODERN INNOVATIONS IN THE TEACHING OF
   READING
  Donald Moyle and Louise M. Moyle
READING READINESS
  John Downing and Derek Thackray
READABILITY
  John Gilliland

Reading: Tests and Assessment Techniques

Peter D. Pumfrey

Senior Lecturer in Education,
University of Manchester

HODDER AND STOUGHTON

for the United Kingdom Reading Association

ISBN 0 340 20067 7 Boards
ISBN 0 340 16554 5 Unibook

Printed in Great Britain for
Hodder and Stoughton Educational,
a division of Hodder and Stoughton Ltd, London,
by T. & A. Constable Ltd, Edinburgh EH7 4NF

Contents

List of figures and tables

Preface

So many books are being published in the education field today that it is very difficult for teachers to keep in touch with research and new developments. This series of monographs has been devised both to collate new ideas and to save teachers of reading from having to spend much of their valuable time searching out relevant texts and materials.

Each monograph will deal with a specific problem area (for example, modern innovations in teaching reading, reading readiness, the development of fluency, problems of assessment), giving a review of theoretical considerations and published research, and pointing out their important practical implications.

Professor J. E. Merritt
Faculty of Educational Studies
The Open University, Milton Keynes

Acknowledgments

I have been greatly helped in the preparation of this monograph by the interest shown by my colleagues in the Department and School of Education of the University of Manchester.

In addition, the work was furthered by the willing cooperation of the many reading test constructors, publishers and distributors whose addresses are given in Appendix 1 of this monograph.

Special mention must be made of Dr R. Sumner and Miss J. M. Hare of the National Foundation for Educational Research in England and Wales; Mrs E. Hutchings, formerly of the Godfrey Thomson Unit for Academic Assessment; Mr F. McBride of Moray House College of Education; Dr W. B. Elley of the New Zealand Council for Educational Research; Mrs J. Eppinger of the Australian Council for Educational Research; and Miss E. MacErlain of the Ontario Institute for Studies in Education. All have given freely of their time in discussing specific reading tests with which they are concerned.

Whilst this work has been greatly facilitated by the above, I must acknowledge the help and encouragement given to me by the General Editor of this series, Professor John Merritt of the Faculty of Educational Studies of the Open University.

Peter D. Pumfrey
Department of Education
University of Manchester

Introduction

Reading tests can make a contribution to the improvement of standards of literacy in our schools. By helping teachers become more aware of children's attainments in and attitudes towards reading, by increasing our understanding of the nature of the reading process and of the specific difficulties faced by many children learning to read, the incidence of reading failure can be reduced.

To use reading tests effectively it is essential that every teacher should be aware of the complexity of the reading process and of the characteristics of reading tests. She must also consider the relationships between the objectives of the reading programme, the methods and materials to be utilised and the assessment of the programme's effectiveness. Thus she needs to be aware of the various uses to which reading tests can be put and of the complementary relationship between the teaching and testing of reading.

These points are considered briefly in this monograph. It is intended primarily as a source of information concerning a selection of reading tests that will be of interest and use to the teacher of any age group of children.

To this end it is in two sections. Section I briefly outlines the justification of the use of reading tests, gives a description of some important dimensions of reading test interpretation and outlines the nature and uses of the informal reading inventory.

Section II gives information about tests available for specified purposes and age ranges of children. The Appendices contain some major sources of information on the testing of reading.

A more extended consideration of important concepts related to the measurement of reading abilities, of both local and national sources of reading test information together with examples of some uses of reading tests is given in a companion volume to this monograph (Pumfrey, in press).* Whilst the monograph and book have a related theme, each publication can be read independently.

* PUMFREY, P. D. (in press) *Measuring Reading Abilities: concepts, sources and applications.* London: Hodder and Stoughton Educational.

In the text which follows, references have been placed at the end of each chapter.

Section I

General Considerations

1 The Uses of Reading Tests

The nature of reading: some considerations

Most of the readers of this monograph will be concerned with teaching children to improve certain aspects of their reading skills. Yet, when asked the deceptively simple question 'What *is* reading?', opinions among teachers (and others) vary greatly. This very question was put in discussion at a recent in-service course for teachers. Results showed that opinions were partly related to the abilities and ages of the children taught, to the length of teaching experience of the teacher and also to the extent that they were aware of current investigations into this topic.

The reading process is far more than a simple, almost mechanical, 'decoding of print to sound' skill whereby the presentation of a flash-card to an infant school child elicits the appropriate oral response. It is more than being able to answer questions on the explicit content of a passage, i.e. 'What was the boy's name in the story you have just read?'. In essence, reading is a constructive thinking process. The competent reader is aware of both the explicit meanings of, for example, proverbs. He can 'read between the lines'. Reading is an active means of information processing. It is both a contributor to and a determinant of cognitive abilities. To argue that modern technology will make reading 'unnecessary' is to misunderstand the nature of the reading process.

Additionally, reading is characteristically developmental. Thus the relative importance of particular skills at a given stage in the development of the abilities characteristic of the competent reader will inevitably vary. The instruction appropriate to an infant is typically different from that required (but rarely given except by 'remedial' teachers) at the secondary or tertiary stages of education. Despite such differences, it should be appreciated that even at the very earliest stage of teaching reading, it is *not* predominantly a mechanical process. One need only ponder the child's tremendous oral language base on which reading is developed, to take the point. From the very start the process of reading is concerned with the extraction of meaning for the child from the printed text.

What is a reading test?

A reading test is a means of determining with some precision the extent to which a child has approached one or more goals of a school's reading instruction programme. Such an instrument may measure attainments in or attitudes towards reading.

The careful selection of the material that comprises a given test enables the user to obtain information economically in terms of her own and her pupil's time. This selection also ensures that the test is valid, reliable and well-organised. Thus reading tests are primarily efficient and valid means of obtaining information. There is no way by which the effectiveness of the teaching of reading can be assessed other than through the use of reading tests of one type or another.

There are many ways in which the teacher may assess reading progress. The familiar standardised, objective reading test is only one type. There are others that are equally, if not more, important.

Objectives, methods and the assessment of reading

The main function of the teacher of reading is to bring about improvements in the pupil's level of reading competence. To be effective, this teaching must be closely related to the rest of the educational programme. Nevertheless, this monograph is deliberately and justifiably focused on the testing of reading.

The changes in performances which the teacher expects her pupils to achieve in reading constitute the goals of her reading programme. It is important that these goals be specified in advance of instruction: it is helpful for a teacher to know explicitly what she expects her pupils to achieve. In my view, the goals should be specified in terms of behaviour that is both *observable* and *measurable*. This requires considerable thought on the part of the teacher. Having specified her objectives in operational terms, however, it is then far easier to select or devise a valid reading test.

In reading, as in any other educational endeavour, objectives, teaching methods and resources and the assessment of the results

of the teaching and learning that have occurred are inter-related aspects that must be considered simultaneously. This is presented diagrammatically in Figure 1.

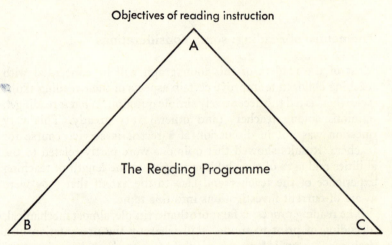

Objectives of reading instruction

A

The Reading Programme

B   C

Methods, resources, curriculum   Assessment of efficacy of B

Figure 1
Essential elements of any reading programme

Why use reading tests?

The purpose in testing reading is to provide the teacher with the information that is needed in order to decide the strategy required to improve the children's reading competencies. This purpose may be achieved in the following six ways.

i. *Finding a starting point for instruction*
If a teacher is faced with a child or a group of children about whose reading abilities she knows little, the use of a reading test can help her decide where to start with them. Knowing the characteristics of a particular age group can help, as also can one's observation and analysis of the children's general behaviour. The use of standardised tests can usefully moderate the first of these and checklists of reading behaviours can do the same for the second. An Informal Reading Inventory (hereafter IRI) can also be used in this situation as can any teacher-constructed test that has been found of value in such circumstances (see Chapter 3, p. 30).

ii. *Comparing reading standards in the class with national norms*
It is easy for a teacher to be unaware of the relative reading attainments and attitudes of her pupils compared with other groups. She might legitimately be concerned with whether the group's scores were in line with national norms or not. It is here that standardised objective tests of reading have much to offer as they will allow such comparisons to be made. Such tests also enable the teacher to judge whether reading standards are changing or not from year to year. However, there is the problem that test content can become more and more out of date each year and changes in reading test scores may reflect this factor rather than genuine differences in reading standards.

iii. *Comparing reading standards of pupils within a class*
It is important for the teacher of reading to be aware of the extent of inter-individual differences in the reading abilities of her pupils. Tests can provide this kind of information and help the teacher to make decisions about how best to organise groups of children for reading instruction.

iv. *Measuring progress in reading*
Progress can be assessed in a number of ways—books read, skills mastered, or gains made *vis à vis* other pupils. The differences between test scores obtained at the start of a period of reading instruction and those obtained at the end provide one quite useful measure. Objective standardised tests can be used for this purpose. Diagnostic tests can be used to assess progress in the mastery of specific skills.

v. *Assessing the effectiveness of various approaches to the teaching of reading*
Reading tests can be used to evaluate the effectiveness of existing practices and of innovations in the teaching of reading. The many schools concerned with the various investigations into the efficacy of the Initial Teaching Alphabet will be well aware of this use of reading tests. Provided that appropriate records are kept, both the short-term and long-term effects of innovations can be objectively appraised. The latter may be particularly important as short-term gains are sometimes achieved at the expense of long-term objectives.

vi. *Diagnosing the reading difficulties of individuals*

Diagnostic reading tests enable the teacher to identify the child's particular skill deficiency as an essential first step in reducing its adverse effects on his reading. Typically, such tests provide a profile of the child's abilities and permit a comparison of relative strengths and weaknesses.

In some instances a child's reading difficulties may be directly attributable to an abnormality of some kind—a disorder or disease of sight or hearing, perhaps. If this can be identified through testing it can often be treated directly and relieve the reading difficulty. However, in the vast majority of cases of difficulties in reading, highly specific causes of this kind cannot be identified. Teachers and researchers are well aware that for almost every child that has a given pattern of strengths and weaknesses in skills purporting to underlie reading ability and who is unable to read, one can find a child with a similar profile who can read proficiently in spite of it.

This points to our incomplete understanding of and control over the development of the ability to read. It also indicates that we must be wary about the conclusions we draw from any diagnosis. To diagnose accurately does not necessarily imply the ability to treat effectively. Nonetheless, diagnostic procedures based on reading tests, though imperfect, provide a valuable point of departure from which to further our understanding of the reading process and our ability to help our pupils to overcome reading difficulties.

A perspective on the six uses of reading tests

The diagnosis of reading difficulties is not an esoteric exercise carried out solely by specialists. It is carried out at many levels. The class teacher is constantly involved in the informal diagnosis of children's reading difficulties. If this approach is not successful, the class teacher may well initiate a more systematic examination of a child's reading difficulties still within the classroom, using a recognised diagnostic reading test, e.g., *The Standard Reading Test Battery*, *Neale Analysis of Reading Ability* (see Section II, pp. 103 and 97). If the child continues to experience difficulties, referral may then be made to someone with more specialised knowledge and expertise such as an educational psychologist or a remedial teacher.

Provided that she is interested in the diagnosis and treatment of reading difficulties, the teacher who notices that a child is having some problem with reading usually asks herself a number of related questions. These might be:

1. What exactly is the child's difficulty?
2. What is causing the problem?
3. Can anything be done to help the child overcome the difficulty?
4. Specifically *what* can I do to help the child?
5. How effective is the help given?
6. How adequate was my original diagnosis?

Diagnostic reading tests can often provide answers to the first question. They can also suggest possible causes of a child's particular difficulty. The answer to the third question is largely determined by the teacher's understanding of reading as a developmental process. Also bearing on it, the manuals of a number of diagnostic reading tests provide general guidelines on the treatment of certain reading problems. However, relatively few provide detailed advice for the teacher on the fourth question. An answer to it is usually dependent on the teacher's ingenuity plus her knowledge of a variety of materials and approaches to skill mastery and motivation. Either informal observation or the use of more systematic testing will meet the fifth question. Any answer to the sixth is usually related to the effectiveness of the teacher's intervention. If it does not enable the child to overcome his difficulty, the original diagnosis may be called into question and the whole series of questions repeated.

During such a revision, the teacher learns more about the nature of the reading process, individual differences between pupils and the effectiveness of a given intervention. She also becomes conscious of the uses and limitations of diagnostic reading tests in assisting her to teach efficiently.

At all levels the diagnosis of reading difficulties is a process of hypothesis generation followed by an intervention, the effects of which lead to a further modification of the hypothesis and thus of the intervention. For example, 'Tommy cannot synthesise simple three- and four-letter phonically regular words; why not? Perhaps it is because . . ., so I will get him to . . . and see whether it will help him cope. If it doesn't, I'll have to think again.'

The following points underlying the diagnosis of reading difficulties should be borne in mind:

 i. Diagnosis is an integral part of effective teaching;

 ii. Diagnosis is intended to facilitate the child's acquisition of specified skills or attitudes;

iii. Diagnosis is not a once-for-all-time activity but is a continuous process in education;

iv. Diagnosis is centred on the individual's particular reading difficulty;

 v. Diagnosis of reading difficulties requires that the teacher be aware of the importance of the other language arts of listening, speaking and writing;

vi. Diagnosis of reading difficulties often requires more than an assessment of cognitive skills as reading difficulties may be symptomatic of a wide range of causative factors;

vii. Diagnosis should involve the use of standardised test procedures where appropriate, but the teacher needs to be aware of the limitations of currently available instruments in this field and to be willing to use other types of tests such as criterion-referenced tests and informal reading tests;

viii. Because our understanding of the reading process is not complete, the diagnosis of a reading difficulty should be based on a pattern of scores, ratings or reading errors;

ix. The heart of diagnosis is the intelligent interpretation of a series of careful, reliable observations coupled with the ability to relate the interpretation to a plan for remedial teaching, and finally;

 x. Only by developing and refining diagnostic procedures can our understanding of the reading process and our ability to prevent and alleviate reading difficulties be furthered.

Who else may need the information reading tests provide?

Whilst the preceding six considerations are likely to be of major interest to the classroom teacher, other people have an interest in the testing of reading. Local Education Authorities (LEAs) might well consider that standardised objective tests of reading provide a useful way of monitoring the extent to which the schools are, or are not, helping to produce a literate population. The results of such testing could also be used when deploying limited resources to places where the need appears greatest. With the facilities currently available for the easy storage and very rapid analysis of such data, there are good reasons for expecting that in the near future all LEAs will have a regular programme of objective testing in the basic subjects at both the primary and secondary level.

Parents generally want their children to become fluent and enthusiastic readers. If their children's schools are sufficiently concerned with their own effectiveness in this respect to test reading regularly, this can be interpreted by parents as explicit recognition of a mutually valued educational objective.

To the pupil of any age the informal and formal testing of reading can help to give a sense of direction. Children and adults generally learn more effectively when they are able to quantify and record their own progress. For example, individual records such as those contained in the SRA Reading Laboratories, the Ward Lock Reading Laboratories and in the Stott *Programmed Reading Kit* Record Card use the impetus provided by knowledge of reading test results to maintain children's motivation to read at a high level.

The testing of reading and related skills forms an important area of educational research. Such research is often criticised because it does not provide the unambiguous and definitive pointers to action that many teachers would like. We all have a tendency to hope for simple answers to complex questions. Reading research is trying to provide us with insights into a phenomenon as complex as anything that man has yet considered.

The teacher as tester

'I've never needed to use a reading test in all my years of teaching reading.' This was a statement made by a primary school teacher who was clearly competent at helping her pupils learn to read. She had taught in the same school for a number of years. The school was one which considered the teaching of reading an important educational objective (as do most schools). Less typically, her pupils were all making excellent, albeit varied, progress in their reading. They also showed considerable and sustained enthusiasm in reading-related activities. It was the type of class that the majority of teachers who had visited described as 'excellently taught', 'a joy to see', 'I'd like my children to attend such a class in such a school'.

Having observed this teacher at work, it was clear that with individual children she was constantly using *informal testing* of their mastery of reading skills. As a result of this information she would modify the content and sequence of learning experiences to which the child was exposed. She also kept a systematic record of the type of difficulties that had been observed, together with comments on the effectiveness of what she had arranged to alleviate the difficulty. However, she did *not* consider this to be 'testing reading'. This excellent teacher had mistakenly identified the process of testing solely with the administration of a particular type of standardised reading test.

The testing of reading is no more than the careful sampling of some important aspects of a child's behaviour related to reading. This testing can be done informally and/or formally. Both aspects of the process are important. They are not mutually exclusive. Even the exceptionally competent teacher of reading is likely to be more effective if she recognises the value of both approaches.

Further reading

(See Appendix 2)

MELNIK, A. and MERRITT, J. (Eds.) (1972) *The Reading Curriculum* Parts III and IV. London: Hodder and Stoughton Educational.

SMITH, F. (1971) *Understanding Reading* New York: Holt, Rinehart and Winston.

SMITH, F. (1973) *Psycholinguistics and Reading* New York: Holt, Rinehart and Winston.

B

2 How can a Reading Test be Selected?

A classification of reading tests

There is a tremendous variety of reading tests and assessment procedures available. It is helpful for the teacher who intends using some to have a conceptual framework within which to classify and think about them. This immediately presents the problem of which characteristics can best be used as a basis for a comprehensive classification? For example, is it helpful to group tests as individual or group, oral or silent, timed or untimed, multiple choice or constructed response? Should tests be grouped according to form, content, age group or method of administration? Important as such points are, to consider these before having thought about the *purpose* for which the test is required, is putting the cart before the horse.

Having established the general purpose, there are three important dimensions that must be considered simultaneously if the teacher is to select a test which will provide the information she requires in the most efficient manner. These dimensions provide a useful framework within which *any* reading test whatsoever may be classified. The dimensions are as follows: firstly, which of the *goals* of the reading programme does the test claim to measure? Secondly, from what kind of *source* is the information collected? Thirdly, what is the level of interpretation to be; that is, to what *use* will the information collected be put?

Each of these dimensions can be sub-divided as follows:

i. The *goals* of the reading programme can be formulated in terms of
 (*a*) attainments (reading skills), and
 (*b*) attitudes towards the activity.

ii. The three major *sources of information* can be described as:
 (*a*) informal tests of reading,
 (*b*) standardised tests of reading, and
 (*c*) criterion-referenced tests of reading.

iii. The *level of interpretation*: basically there are the following three levels of reading test interpretation, each level related to different uses:
 (*a*) descriptive,
 (*b*) diagnostic: (1) historic, (2) predictive, and
 (*c*) evaluative.

These three major aspects (i, ii and iii) of reading tests can be represented visually as in Figure 2. A further consideration of these three dimensions will help to clarify a number of points that are central to the effective use of reading tests by the teacher.

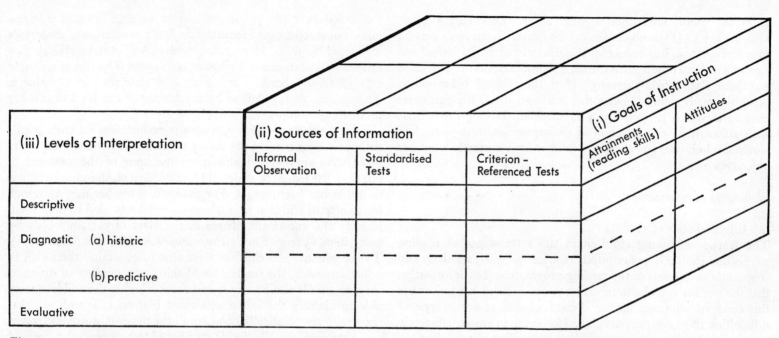

Figure 2

Model for the classification of reading tests in relation to objectives of reading instruction, sources of information and levels of interpretation

i. *Goals*

Most teachers of reading would agree that two of their aims are 'To enable every child to become a competent reader' and 'To enable every child to obtain pleasure from reading'. The disadvantage of goals expressed in this way is that it is difficult to assess the extent to which they have been achieved. It is important that the goals of the reading programme be defined in terms of objectives that can be observed, taught and/or learned, and measured.

To define goals in this way is a far from easy task. However, there are useful guidelines to help the teacher (Vargas 1972; Wallen 1972).* Thus objectives can be broken down from general to specific ones. For example, the operational definition of *one part* of a general objective in the cognitive area could be 'The child can *name* flash cards correctly'. Here the type of behaviour is unambiguously defined. Once this has been done, the particular content to which it applies can be specified. Having carried out such an analysis, the selection of an appropriate test of reading is made much easier because the teacher knows exactly what her objectives are.

ii. *Sources of information*

(*a*) Informal tests of reading

The teacher of young children in the early stages of reading acquisition should hear her pupils read individually, regularly and frequently as *one part* of the reading programme. The information that the teacher can obtain in such a situation helps her to identify the children who are having difficulties and also the type of difficulties they are experiencing. However, to do so efficiently requires that the teacher use an adequate method of recording the child's responses and analysing error patterns. The error pattern will suggest ways of helping the child and, at an informal level, the teacher can then evaluate the efficacy of whatever interventions she puts in train. Such informal analyses and records mean that the teacher is more likely *consciously* to recognise important diagnostic indicators and constructive ways of responding to

them. She becomes less dependent on an intuitive and unsystematic approach to the identification and remediation of children's reading difficulties. Her professional expertise is increased. She can communicate her activities to colleagues. The use of a simple type of error recording and analysis is described in Chapter 3. The system can be adapted by any teacher at any level to suit her particular requirements.

Most teachers readily make up attainment tests for their pupils without having studied the theory of test construction. Frequently these tests are devised almost on the spur of the moment to establish the extent to which the pupils have mastered a particular skill that has been taught. For example, a teacher might arrange for groups of children to work on material intended to help them identify the consonant blends at the start of certain words by using item 15 from Stott's *Programmed Reading Kit* (Stott 1971). To see whether the children were able to generalise their skill to other situations, the teacher could think of a number of different yet structurally similar words and check whether the children were able to identify the initial consonant blends. It is unlikely that she would systematically consider all the possible words she might use, but would rapidly decide on a list of twenty or so that seemed to her pertinent to the skill she wished to test. The informality in the construction, administration and interpretation of such tests is readily apparent. Their major strength lies in the skill of the teacher in choosing valid items.

Currently there is a move to help teachers construct rather more adequate attainment tests in areas such as reading. The Educational Testing Service, Princeton, New Jersey, publish two small pamphlets called 'Making a Classroom Test—A Guide for

* Full references are given at the end of the chapter.

Teachers' and 'Short-cut Statistics for Teacher-made Tests'. These can be obtained for a nominal sum. They tend to emphasise the considerations normally borne in mind by test constructors when making up a standardised test, but are still of value to the teacher interested in ensuring that her own informal classroom tests are good ones.

Quite useful reading comprehension tests can be readily constructed using the 'cloze' technique (Moyle 1972). All that is required here is to take an appropriate passage and block out some of the words. The child's task is to read the passage and deduce the missing words from the context. The same technique is also used in both standardised and criterion-referenced reading tests (e.g. *GAP Reading Comprehension Test*, Section II).

The Informal Reading Inventory (IRI) is described at length in Chapter 3, because it is an important assessment procedure for the classroom teacher bringing the strengths of informal and criterion-referenced testing together. It is considered by the author as one of the most promising approaches to assessment available to the teacher of reading.

The use of reading tests by a teacher means that careful observation of the pupil's reading behaviours can take place. Such observations, if systematic, planned, recorded, analysed and their interpretation acted upon, can enable the teacher to assess reading competencies, to measure progress and to diagnose difficulties.

(b) Standardised tests of reading

The two most important characteristics of standardised tests are that they have been designed to discriminate between children and their norms are established on a specified group. Their use enables the teacher to answer questions such as 'Is Peter's reading comprehension ability using a multiple choice test superior to John's?' The distinction between the informal test, which also is able to provide an answer to this question, and the formal *standardised* test is that the latter gives an answer with a known degree of precision. Children can be compared with their immediate peers and also with the scores of the sample on whom the test has been standardised.

A refinement of this approach leads to the standardised diagnostic reading test. This type of test can give a number of scores for the individual child on different aspects of the reading process. These scores are sometimes presented in the form of a profile from which the diagnosis of areas of difficulty can be made and ideas for remedial work generated. For example, the *Neale Analysis of Reading Ability* (see Section II) gives scores for speed, accuracy and comprehension. It also provides an analysis of the specific reading errors made by the child.

The interpretation of standardised reading test profiles is a complex subject. It is discussed in the companion volume to this monograph. An understanding of the reliabilities of the sub-test scores and of their intercorrelations is necessary if a profile is to be interpreted adequately (Pumfrey, in press).

National surveys of reading are based on standardised objective tests. For example, the *Southgate Group Reading Tests* 1 and 2 (see Section II) and various of the standardised tests produced by the NFER have been used extensively. This type of test is extremely important, but it should not blind the teacher to the availability of other sources of information that may be more appropriate to her pupil's needs and her school's resources. It must be borne in mind also that many standardised objective reading tests are very limited in the range of skills they measure.

(c) Criterion-referenced tests of reading

Some tests of reading are based on the premise that *all* children need to master certain reading skills if they are to cope adequately with skills at progressively higher levels of complexity. The focus of attention is *not* on the individual differences between children, but on a comparison of the child's abilities in relation to that level which it is deemed reasonable and necessary that he achieve. For example, it might be considered that *all* children need to be able to recognise the twelve words in English that comprise about one quarter of typical written material (McNally and Murray 1962). Immediate recognition of these twelve words can be regarded as a criterion of reading performance. The teacher is concerned that *all* children achieve this goal and is not particularly interested in the fact that, if they do, the twelve-word test no longer serves to help her to discriminate between the children in terms of relative ability. Similarly, the headmistress of an Infants' school who aims to have all children reading *at least* to a certain book in a graded series, is stressing a criterion goal.

Criterion-referenced tests are primarily concerned with the child's ability to cope with items representative of a specified criterion of reading competence. Such tests are usually made up on the basis of a detailed analysis of the content of reading instruction. Jackson's *Phonic Skills Tests* is an example (see Section II, Chapter 4) of this type of test. Many of the diagnostic reading tests contained in the handbook by Daniels and Diack (1970) are also criterion-referenced tests. The tremendous popularity of this battery of tests suggests that many practising teachers find them helpful in diagnosing difficulties.

The criterion-referenced approach to the testing of reading is built into some graded reading series such as the series *Programmed Reading* by McGraw-Hill. In these books a test of the material covered forms an integral part of the programme. It must be coped with adequately before the child proceeds to a more advanced level of work. The same is true of the Macmillan Reading Programme and Sipay's *Mastery Tests* (see Section II).

One further homely example might help clarify the concept of criterion-referenced measurement for those to whom it is unfamiliar. At the back of many books in series of graded readers there is a list of the words used in the reader. When a child comes to the teacher saying that he has finished reading the book and asking if he can go on to the next one in the series, after checking that the child has understood the story, the teacher typically asks the child to read the 'out of context' list of words at the back of the book. If the child can read them, he is given the next book in the series. If he cannot, he is usually referred to another book of similar level to that which he claims to have completed, or certain work is prescribed on the basis of the material he obviously has not mastered. This is using the 'out of context' words as a criterion-referenced test based on a content analysis of the reader.

The criterion-referenced test of reading is related to the informal approaches that can be used by the teacher in the closeness of its link with the child's reading programme. It is a move away from the normative standardised test approach. Currently a number of criterion-referenced reading tests are being developed and there are sound reasons for teachers welcoming such instruments.

At the same time it should be remembered that any criterion-referenced reading test such as the Dolch *Basic Sight Word Test* inevitably has a normative aspect in the same way that any normative test has a criterion-referenced one. For this reason, some test constructors have tried to combine the advantages of criterion-referenced measurement of reading skills with normative scores e.g. the *Woodcock Reading Mastery Tests* (see Section II, Chapter 4).

iii. *Level of interpretation*
It was suggested earlier that interpretation of the information obtained from any reading test or assessment procedure can be considered at three major levels:
(*a*) descriptive,
(*b*) diagnostic: (1) historic, (2) predictive; and
(*c*) evaluative.

The first level, *descriptive*, merely enables the situation as it is now to be described with some precision. It is frequently found in official reports and surveys.

The second, *diagnostic*, is of much more importance to the teacher. It has two aspects, the historic and the predictive. The former is concerned with the possible causes of a child's current pattern of reading competencies. The latter is forward looking. It is concerned with the interpretation of findings in terms of planning some kind of instructional programme to take the child on to the next stage of reading development.

Interpretation of information at the level of *evaluation* involves considering the effectiveness of the reading programme in the context of the overall values of the teacher and the school and the resources available to help achieve the various goals of the curriculum. For example, how important is it that children should read and enjoy the activity? Are there not other educational goals of equal importance? What resources, in terms of teacher, and pupil time and school capitation allowance should be allocated to the teaching and learning of reading? What improvements might reasonably be effected?

In practice the teacher moves rapidly between these three levels of interpretation. Any reading test can be used at any level but some tests are more appropriate to one than the others.

If John obtains a reading age of six years on a reading test, that is a descriptive statement. If the teacher looks at the pattern of errors in his responses and at the boy's situation in general, she is shifting her level of interpretation to diagnosis, either historic and/or (more usefully) predictive. If the teacher then questions the efficacy of the reading programme, her goals and the resources that are brought to bear on achieving them, the information obtained from the reading test or other assessment procedure is being considered in a much wider sense. It is being used evaluatively.

It is not unknown for teachers to say of reading tests 'It's not what I really wanted, but it is the only one available at our school'. Or even worse, 'I only know of one reading test' (usually the Schonell *Graded Word Reading Test* or the *Burt (rearranged) Word Reading Test*). These are two examples of test selection determined by relatively unimportant considerations. If the proposed three-dimensional model is applied, the teacher is more likely to be able to select appropriately from the vast array of reading tests and assessment procedures available those which are best suited to her particular purpose.

Using the three dimensions

The value when thinking about reading tests of using the three dimensions given in Figure 2 is shown in the following two typical teaching situations.

A teacher might ask 'How do the reading standards of my class compare with national norms?' Here she is interested in the goal of *attainment* in certain reading skills. The source of information most appropriate would be a nationally *standardised test* of the reading skill or skills under consideration. The initial emphasis of interpretation would be *descriptive*.

When thinking about arranging appropriate word-attack experiences for a child, the teacher may wonder precisely where a pupil's knowledge of phonics is weak. Here also her concern is with the goal of *attainment*. The source of information could be a *criterion-referenced test* such as Jackson's *Phonic Skills Tests* (see Section II). In this instance the emphasis of interpretation is *diagnostic*.

In Tables 5 and 6, pp. 43 and 44, the reading tests described in Section II of this monograph have been categorised according to the model described. It is anticipated that this will help the teacher to locate reading tests or assessment procedures that will suit these varied purposes for children of different age groups.

Important characteristics of reading tests

Once the teacher has decided on the *kind* of reading test needed to suit the particular purpose, the next task is to identify a suitable test. It is important, therefore, to understand certain characteristics of the tests themselves.

The three most important characteristics of any reading test are validity, reliability and practicability. The *validity* of a test indicates the extent to which it measures that which it is intended to measure. Its *reliability* describes the degree to which the instrument produces consistent results. Its *practicability* is concerned with the extent to which a particular instrument is of use to the teacher in her particular school situation.

It is possible to have a highly reliable reading test that is not valid for a particular purpose. For example, a test of reading comprehension can give very reliable results, but if the focus of the teacher's interest is on children's rate of reading a particular type of material, the comprehension test is unlikely to be a valid measure of her particular objective. High reliability does *not* guarantee validity. However, if a reading test can be shown to have high validity, it must have high reliability. By analogy, if I have a wrist watch which keeps excellent time, it is highly reliable. If, however, it stops and I wind it up without resetting the hands, it is still a reliable instrument but the information it provides concerning time is no longer valid. In selecting a reading test the first consideration should be its validity.

Strictly speaking, it is more accurate to talk about the validities and reliabilities of reading tests, although for convenience these terms are often referred to collectively. Each can be expressed with considerable precision in relation to the vast majority of standardised tests of reading but the concepts apply to information obtained from *any* source.

i. *Validities*

The four types of validity most commonly mentioned in reading test manuals are *content*, *concurrent*, *predictive* and *construct* validity.

Content validity is indicated by the extent to which the items comprising the test form a satisfactory sample of items which actually tap the ability the test constructor wishes to measure. For example, if a test is of phonically regular three-letter words, does it adequately sample the universe of such words appropriate to the age level for whom the test is intended? The constructors of reading tests should give potential users evidence of the test's content validity. The responsibility is then on the teacher to decide whether the given test is appropriate for her particular purpose.

Evidence of *concurrent validity* is often presented by showing the extent to which the scores on a reading test relate to other measures of current reading performance by the same group of children. For example, the correlation between scores on an established and a newly constructed word reading test might be calculated to provide one index of concurrent validity for the new test. Thus, if children who do well on the new *Marino Graded Word Reading Scale* do well on the old Burt Test, and those who find difficulty with the new one also find the old test hard, this information could be presented as evidence of concurrent validity. Similarly the teacher's subjective ranking of children in word reading skill could be correlated with the same children's scores on a word reading test. A high relationship could be interpreted as further evidence of concurrent validity.

Information describing the validities of a reading test (other than content validity) is commonly presented as indices ranging from 0 to 1, the former indicating zero validity and the latter perfect validity. In practice no test is completely valid.

Predictive validity of a reading test is concerned with the extent that a test will predict children's future reading competencies. For example, children who are poor readers at the age of eight years as measured by a reading comprehension test are likely to remain *relatively* poor readers even at the end of their secondary school careers. Of course, there will be individual children who will not conform to this prediction. The aim of the teacher is firstly to recognise such predictive validity and secondly to seek to invalidate it. She can do this by diagnosing likely causes of a child's relative failure and attempting to reduce them by appropriate intervention. In some cases, the improvement of a child's reading competencies can be achieved without recourse to any reading material. This could occur if an extremely anxious child was helped, through therapy, to come to terms with his emotional problems. He could then channel his energies towards the mastery and enjoyments of reading.

Construct validity is concerned with the test constructor showing that the items of the test are an adequate sample of the behaviours included in whatever theoretical psychological attributes the particular reading test is designed to measure. If, for example, it is claimed that a test is measuring some kind of comprehension, the text constructor must provide reasonable grounds for supposing that such psychological processes exist and that the test provides a valid measure of them.

ii. *Reliabilities*

To be valid, reading tests must be reliable. Indeed, test reliability puts a ceiling on the validity that can be expected. In general, no test can have a validity higher than the square root of its reliability. The reliability of a test is frequently expressed as a coefficient of the same kind as the correlation coefficient. It ranges from 0 to 1, where the former indicates complete unreliability and the latter complete reliability. The four major reliability coefficients pertinent to the selection of a reading test are those of *stability*, *equivalence*, *internal consistency* and a combination of *stability and equivalence*.

The *stability* of a reading test is estimated by administering it twice to a group of children. For this reason it is often referred to as 'test-retest reliability'. The agreement between the two sets of scores obtained is then calculated. If the children's scores do not vary greatly from one occasion to the next, the test-retest reliability is said to be high.

In some reading tests, for example the *Southgate Group Reading Tests* 1 and 2 (see Section II), there are parallel forms of the tests. This makes it possible to test the same skill on *equivalent* but different material. The relationship between children's scores on the administration of two such parallel forms of a test is called the coefficient of equivalence.

When parallel forms are not available and it is not practical to test children twice on the same test, techniques have been devised enabling an estimate of reliability to be achieved from only one administration of a reading test. This is sometimes done by giving the test to a group of children and then dividing the items of the test into two sets, for example on the basis of odd and even items. Thus each child has a score on the odd items and another on the even items. The relationship between these sets of scores for the group can then be calculated. The resultant correlation is called a coefficient of *internal consistency*.

Finally, when a parallel form of a test is administered after a period of time, a coefficient of *stability and equivalence* can be calculated. Generally, such coefficients are rather lower than those obtained from other methods of calculating reliability.

Reading test manuals do not usually contain all of the above indices. The coefficient that is of interest to the teacher is the one that is most pertinent to her purpose in using the test. It is not necessarily the test with the highest coefficient of reliability that is the most appropriate. Because of this, it is difficult to prescribe arbitrary standards concerning the minimum acceptable reliabilities of reading tests. The NFER suggest that the minimum internal consistency reliability coefficients for attainment tests including tests of reading should be ·85 for stability and ·9 for internal consistency. However, there are different acceptable levels dependent on the type of decision one will have to make. Levels of reliability below those given here can be tolerated in certain circumstances (Pumfrey, in press).

Another way of thinking about the meaning of reliability is in terms of the extent to which children's scores vary from time to time for any number of reasons. In one sense the score that a child obtains on a reading test can be considered as made up of two elements. There is that part which represents his 'true' score and a part representing the host of variables that can either raise or depress the score he obtains. This latter part is often referred to as 'error'. Illness, or having read some related material first before a test, could be chance influences that would affect the obtained score. In the first instance it would probably reduce the obtained score; and in the second increase it. If changes in reading test scores are not large between successive testings, the effects of extraneous variables are small and the test is reliable. If a child's score changed from say, a reading age of seven years to one of thirteen years on a test given twice over a period of a week and there appeared to be no valid reason for the change, one would have considerable doubts as to the reliability of such an instrument.

In fact, the extent to which a child's obtained score on a test is likely to differ from an estimate of his 'true' score can be calculated for any particular test. The extent of this variation in obtained scores is often expressed as the standard error of measurement. The smaller the standard error of a test, the more reliable it is. For example, in the NFER *Reading Test AD* (formerly *Sentence Reading Test 1*), a standard error of 2·7 points is quoted for the age group 8 years 2 months to 9 years 1 month. This indicates that a child's obtained score will, by chance, only vary from his 'true' score by plus or minus twice the standard error of measurement once in twenty times. The test-retest reliability of this particular instrument is 0·97.

The most valuable source of information concerning any satisfactory reading test is the handbook which accompanies it. It should always be read carefully and critically before using any test. Many manuals contain relatively sparse details about validities, reliabilities and standardisation. Fortunately the situation is improving. Teachers are becoming more appreciative of the value of a good manual such as those usually produced by the NFER. The content of manuals can be expected to improve in line with the criteria that have been spelled out by the British Psychological Society (1960).

It is also useful to read critical reviews of reading tests if one wishes to be aware of their weaknesses. The best source of such reports is in the Buros Mental Measurement Yearbooks (e.g. Buros 1972) and the associated handbook *Reading Tests and Reviews* (Buros 1968). In 1974 Buros published a compendium listing all tests in print, including recently published reading tests (Buros 1974). The major disadvantage of such books is that they can never be completely up to date with new tests that are being produced. For evaluations of more recent tests it is useful to consult periodicals produced by organisations such as the International Reading Association, the United Kingdom Reading Association and the National Association for Remedial Education. Their addresses are given in Appendix 1.

iii. *Practicability*

The most important characteristic of any reading test is that it must be suited to the particular purpose determined by the teacher. Within this limitation, for tests of similar validities and reliabilities, the following five practical considerations loom large:

1. Is the reading test readily available?
2. Am I able to administer the test?
3. Can I interpret the results?
4. How much time will its use entail?
5. Is it expensive to use?

These questions require considerable thought and in some cases result in a teacher making up her mind to acquire the knowledge and competencies needed if she is to use certain instruments (Pumfrey, in press).

With reference to questions 1, 2 and 3, reading tests vary greatly in their complexity. Because of this, all reading tests are not openly available to all teachers. However, the vast majority of these instruments are available to teachers through their schools. The NFER classifies the reading tests it issues into the following five major levels (NFER 1975).

Level A Tests: includes any objectively scored attainment test and inventory requiring relatively limited technical knowledge for its use. These include all the tests of reading in their catalogue *Tests for Guidance and Assessment.*

Level P Tests: the user of these tests needs to have completed satisfactorily a course of training in test administration and interpretation, or had equivalent experience under the supervision of a trained and qualified psychologist.

Level Q Tests: these are available to individuals having a thorough knowledge of the theory of testing, considerable practical experience *plus* training in the particular test.

Level R Tests: at this level users require a very substantial background in the theory and practice of mental measurement at the post-graduate level.

Level K Tests: these are clinical instruments sometimes used in studying certain pathological conditions. Interpreting the results of such tests is largely dependent on the clinical judgment of the user. Typically she would be a qualified educational psychologist, clinical psychologist or psychiatrist. Additionally, users must have had specific training in the uses of the test.

The sequence A, P, Q, R, K indicates tests of increasing complexity. The tests described in Section II are classified in line with the above system.

Whilst some teachers might question the above restrictions in test availability, teachers sufficiently interested can acquire the testing and diagnostic expertise and knowledge required. Indeed, their initial training often contains a course on mental measurement and testing.

The vast majority of reading tests are available to most teachers. Not all test distributors are as restrictive (rightly or wrongly) as the NFER.

Records

Each school should have a recognised testing and assessment programme in which reading competencies figure prominently. Within the programme individual teachers can be encouraged to develop their individual testing and assessment expertise with the pupils for whom they have responsibility.

At both levels records should be kept so that both group and individual trends in reading progress can be identified. This information will enable such action as is deemed necessary to be taken on the basis of evidence rather than opinion.

For each individual child a cumulative record of his reading test results should be kept. There are good educational reasons for encouraging pupils to maintain these records themselves. Such records can be of great value to the teacher (and her pupils) in these days of rapid staff changes. The records should also be transferable to successive schools. In this respect the Armed

Forces Educational Services are far ahead of their civilian colleagues.

References

British Psychological Society (1960). 'Technical recommendations for psychological and educational tests prepared by the Committee on Test Standards of the British Psychological Society', *British Psychological Society Bulletin*, 41, 13-17.

BUROS, O. K. (Ed.) (1968) *Reading Tests and Reviews* New Jersey: Gryphon Press.

BUROS, O. K. (Ed.) (1972) *The Seventh Mental Measurement Yearbook* New Jersey: Gryphon Press.

BUROS, O. K. (Ed.) (1974) *Tests in Print II* New Jersey: Gryphon Press, 2nd edit.

DANIELS, J. C. and DIACK, H. (1970) *The Standard Reading Tests* London: Chatto and Windus, 7th impression.

MOYLE, D. (1972) 'Readability—the use of cloze procedure'. In MELNIK, A. and MERRITT, J. (Eds.), *The Reading Curriculum* London: Hodder and Stoughton Educational in association with the Open University Press.

National Foundation for Educational Research (1975) *Test Catalogue* Slough: NFER.

PUMFREY, P. D. (in press) *Measuring Reading Abilities: Concepts, Sources and Applications* London: Hodder and Stoughton Educational.

STOTT, D. H. (1971) *Programmed Reading Kit* Edinburgh: Holmes McDougall.

WALLEN, C. J. (1972) *Competency in Teaching Reading* Henley: Science Research Associates.

VARGUS, J. S. (1972) *Writing Worthwhile Behavioural Objectives* London: Harper and Row.

Further reading

(See Section II, Appendix 2)

Books with the number 1 before the author's name are likely to be particularly helpful to any reader wishing to pursue further the topics touched on in this chapter.

3 The Informal Reading Inventory

Definition of reading levels

From the point of view of the teacher, each pupil can be considered as having not one but a number of reading age levels. A child's level of reading proficiency is related to his abilities, the nature of the reading task he faces and his interest in it. Following the work of Johnson and Kress (1972), it is helpful to distinguish between four levels of reading skill:

Independent level: This is the level at which a child can read with fluency, understanding, accuracy and enjoyment. It is the level at which he can deal with reading material without requiring supervision or help. The material is seen by the child as 'easy to read'. The over-learning essential to proficient reading requires much experience at this level.

Instructional level: At this level the child can benefit from systematic instruction by a teacher. The material is seen by the child as presenting some difficulties with which he will need help but much of the material will be within his grasp.

Frustration level: Any material which is so difficult that the child makes many errors, is slow, hesitant, cannot readily understand the meaning and from which he can be easily distracted, can be considered as presenting him with a frustrating experience. At this difficulty level the chances of a child improving his reading skills and attitudes towards reading are virtually nil. The material is seen as distasteful and to be avoided.

Capacity level: Whilst the estimation of the level at which a child might be expected to read is exceedingly complex, a pupil's ability to listen to and comprehend orally presented material can form a useful index of reading potential. The child is tested to see whether when questioned on such material, he understands *and* shows an oral language level in line with the level of the material that has been read to him.

Estimates of these four levels can be obtained by administering an Informal Reading Inventory (IRI).

The concept of an inventory means that both attainments in and attitudes towards reading as well as any pertinent aspect of language development can be considered. It is an informal reading test in the sense that a wide variety of unstandardised materials can be used in an IRI, and there is no normative comparison with what other students can do. The child's performance is compared with a defined criterion of *mastery* of reading rather than by considering how much more or less capable he is than his peers.

Such an inventory is *not* informal in its procedures. The central aim is to identify whether a text, from which a teacher wishes a child to work, is suited to the child's reading skills and is not too difficult for the child. *This applies irrespective of the subject concerned or the level of complexity of the material.* Thus the technique is of importance to *any* teacher of *any* subject at *any* level where the child's study involves dealing with textual material.

The IRI is based on the assumption that reading attainments follow a developmental pattern analogous to aspects of physical development such as height, weight or size of feet. To determine whether a shoe 'fits', the common sense approach is to try it on. Similarly, to establish whether or not a book 'fits' a child, the child should try to read it. The IRI systematises the teacher's observation of how well particular reading material suits a child. To be able to recommend the appropriate book for a child, i.e. at either the Independent or Instructional level, is central to success in the teaching of reading.

The definition of the reading attainments appropriate to each of the levels described is given in Table 1. The figures presented are based on the consensus of expert opinion in the field. The percentages indicate the degree of success typifying the various levels in relation to different aspects of reading.

It is interesting to note that the class teacher *frequently underestimates* the difficulty level of the reading material with which her children are faced. The use of an IRI makes one immediately aware of discrepancies between teacher estimation of the difficulty level of textual material and the actual difficulty level experienced by the child. Too many pupils spend too much time with textual material which is at Frustration level.

The core of an IRI comprises a series of graded passages of writing which the child is asked to read aloud (or silently). After each passage he is questioned about it. It is usual to select passages from a graded basal reading series not known to the child, or from graded material such as that contained in a reading laboratory. If she so wishes, the teacher can use her own material.

In all instances it is important that the content of the material be pertinent to the child's interests, otherwise low achievement can be confused with poor effort. The lengths of the passages or block of words selected for reading should be about 20 words at the pre-primer level and gradually increased in length from more difficult texts by amounts which keep the calculation of the percentages given in Table 1 easy, i.e. use passages or blocks of 20, 40, 60, 80, or 100 words. The questions asked to test the child's understanding of the material should include different levels of comprehension. Thus questions concerning word meaning, questions of fact, questions concerning the main ideas contained in the passage and, where appropriate, questions concerning inferences and implications will be asked. Valmont (1972) gives a useful guide to the construction of suitable questions.

Thus the child might, for example, be asked to read aloud passages from graded material such as a series of basal readers beginning at an easy level (independent) and continuing until the material is too difficult for the child according to the criteria given for Frustration level.

The teacher will need a prepared copy of the passages being read. The accuracy of the child and his ability to comprehend what is being read can be recorded. The child's errors can be easily recorded, analysed and (more difficult) their implications

Table 1

Suggested criteria for assessing some achievements using an Informal Reading Inventory

Reading Level	Skills Tested						
	Oral Reading Accuracy			Reading Comprehension		Rate of Reading	
	a. Words in isolation		*b.* Words in context	*c.* Definition of words out of context (text removed)	*d.* Answering questions using contextual cues (text available)	*e.* Oral	*f.* Silent
	i. flash presentation (i.e. ½″ exposure)	ii. untimed					
Independent Level	90%-100%	95%-100%	99%-100%	90%-100%	90%-100%	Oral reading about half the rate of silent reading for same level of comprehension	
Instructional Level	50%-89%	60%-94%	95%-98%	60%-89%	70%-89%	Oral reading rate equal to or not more than 15 words per minute *less* than silent reading	
Frustration Level	Below 50%	Below 60%	Below 95%	Below 60%	Below 70%	Oral reading faster than silent reading by up to 15 words per minute	
Capacity Level					Listening comprehension of 75% of material		

for reading instruction considered. An IRI can also be constructed from groups of 'out of context' words of progressively greater difficulty which can be read either orally and/or silently and the child's attainments summarised as in Table 2.

The child's rate of reading can also be observed. If the child's rate of oral reading is very, very slow it is highly likely that the material represents a frustrating experience for the child, especially if the material is too lengthy. It has been argued by McCracken (1971) that rate of oral reading itself does not *alone* determine that material is frustrating for a child unless his silent reading is much slower, given that the understanding of the material is equivalent under both conditions.

It should be noted that if *any one* of the skills tested is at the level of Frustration, then the material is Frustration level for the child even if the child's other indices all indicate higher levels.

Group IRIs

Informal Reading Inventories can readily be adapted for use with groups of pupils of any age and level of ability. A group IRI may be used to assess the extent to which a child had understood a given passage of writing. It might also allow an appraisal of the extent to which the pupil was using appropriate techniques in situations requiring different reading skills.

The former consideration would necessitate the teacher devising questions on the meaning of the vocabulary used in the passage, as well as other aspects of reading comprehension. The first of these might be tested by requiring the child to select suitable synonyms or antonyms of given words, or to use a dictionary to establish the meaning of particular words. Other aspects of reading comprehension such as the pupil's ability to identify the main ideas in a passage of writing, to note the sequence of ideas, to show understanding of particular points of explicit meaning, to comment on implicit meanings and to draw conclusions could be tested by setting suitable questions. The second focus of concern, namely the pupil's ability to use differing reading techniques appropriately, could be examined by setting tasks that require the reader to use, for example, 'skimming' or other rapid reading techniques and other tasks that require close attention to detail.

An IRI can also be used by the teacher to check that readers are able to use the various parts of a book effectively. For example, the use of the table of contents, the subject index, the author index and the glossary can readily be tested by framing suitable questions. Attitudes to reading can be measured using IRIs by, for instance, getting a pupil to report on the extent to which he enjoys reading materials of various types using a simple five-point rating scale. The frequency with which a pupil uses the class, school or local library facilities can be recorded.

Thus both objective type comprehension questions about which there is no doubt as to the correct answer and subjective estimates such as pupil and teacher ratings can be incorporated in the same IRI. Facts about reading comprehension can be compared with, say, the pupil's opinion of his own reading ability. The comparison by the teacher of her rating of the pupil on the same dimension can be most helpful in reducing misunderstanding between pupil and teacher. Currently, in writing end-of-term school reports, some schools include space for *both* pupils and teachers to record their comments on work done. Such a scheme

C

Table 2
Summarising children's responses to teacher-devised IRIs*

Name: John Smith   *Date:* 21st September 1975   *Age:* 8 years   *Examiner:* T. Cher

A. IRI Results

Material or Book Level	Oral Reading Accuracy			Reading Comprehension		Listening Comprehension	Rate of Reading	
	a. Words in isolation		b. Words in context	c. Definition of words out of context	d. Answering questions using contextual cues (silent reading)		e. Oral	f. Silent
	i. flash presentation (i.e. $\frac{1}{2}''$ exposure)	ii. untimed						
Pre-Primer	100%	100%	99%	95%	95%		70	75
Primer	90%	95%	99%	90%	90%		60	65
Book 1	80%	85%	95%	80%	80%		50	50
Book 2	70%	65%	80% (F)	65%	85%	90%	40	30
Book 3	40% (F)	48% (F)	75% (F)	50% (F)	75%	85%		
Book 4						80% (C)		
Book 5						60%		

Table 2 *contd.*

B. Pupil's Reading Levels		C. Significant Error Patterns	D. Action to be Taken
Independent	Primer	(Obtained from a consideration of	(Based on interpretation
Instructional	1	John's responses to the IRI	of B and C)
Frustration	2	materials—see Table 4, page 38,	
Listening Comprehension		for an example.)	
(i.e. 'Capacity')	4		

* (i) Though here we are concerned mainly with attainments, *any* aspect of reading behaviour can be incorporated into an IRI, including rating of attitudes or other aspects of behaviour.
  (ii) IRIs can be constructed from material at *any* level of difficulty from kindergarten to tertiary education.
  (iii) IRIs are constructed by the teacher to suit her situation: thus it would be unlikely that all children in a normal class would be assessed on *all* the aspects of reading shown above.
  (iv) The more competent the reader, the greater the emphasis in an IRI on various aspects of silent reading comprehension.

has much to commend it. The approach can readily be built into an IRI as one part of the continuous assessment of a reading programme. All pupils can be encouraged to maintain, in part, their own records of reading progress.

The results of any Group IRI can be rapidly summarised by listing the reading skills tested at the head of a series of columns. The names of the children can be listed down the left hand side of the record sheet. If the teacher marks with a tick those aspects of reading in which each child is reaching a satisfactory criterion, her group summary sheet will provide a diagnostic pattern. This pattern will enable her to identify rapidly the reading skills in which, as a group, her pupils' need of instruction is greatest.

The scope of the IRI is virtually unlimited. Its flexibility is its greatest strength. A teacher-constructed IRI can include *any* reading programme objective that she considers important. As a technique the IRI allows the teacher to use her critical judgment and imagination in devising methods of monitoring the effectiveness of the reading programme that both she and her pupils find rewarding.

Error analysis

Many teachers of reading hear children read orally and individually as one aspect of the reading programme. Frequently all that is recorded is a date and page number on a book marker. The child is merely given 'practice', with such help as seems appropriate at the time. With minimal effort on the teacher's part, a much greater return can be achieved from the session with the child.

On the reasonable assumption that a child's oral reading errors are caused and are not fortuitous, the discrepancies between the child's observed oral response and the expected response (on the basis of 100 per cent accuracy) allows the teacher an opportunity of noting patterns of errors and forming diagnostic hypotheses.

If the teacher systematises her observations of the child's reading and is able to record certain types of errors, she is likely to see a pattern of errors appear. From this *pattern*, appropriate remedial measures can be devised. For example, if the pattern of errors showed a high level of reversals (e.g. 'no' for 'on'; 'was' for 'saw') various ways might be sought to help the child make the necessary discriminations. If, on the other hand, the teacher's observations had not been systematised, it is highly likely that the pattern of a child's errors would never have become sufficiently clear to the teacher to enable her to plan appropriate learning.

In his research Christenson (1969) looked at the types and frequencies of errors made by children using an IRI based on a graded reading series. The following seven types of errors were considered:

omissions
substitutions
additions
refusals
repetitions
reversals and
gross mispronunciations.

It was found that the type of error produced was related to the reading level of the material. Errors of repetition occur more often at the Independent level. Mispronunciations, refusals and substitutions were more typical of the Frustration level. At the Frustration level, boys tend to substitute words whereas girls waited to be prompted. Characteristic differences also appeared between the Instructional level and the Frustration level. Thus error pattern is closely related to the level of difficulty of the material.

A good ten-year-old reader will make virtually no errors when reading from say, *Wide Range Readers Green Book* 1 or 2. He will begin to make repetitions as the difficulty of the material increases. With reading material at the eleven to twelve-year-old level, he will begin to make substitutions and corrections but he will tend to correct these errors. At the thirteen to fourteen-year-old level he meets unknown words, makes omissions, mispronunciations and does not correct his errors.

Error analysis is most usefully carried out with reading materials at the Instructional level for obvious reasons. The types of errors and the patterns of errors recorded by a teacher help her to link effective interventions with them, for children of given characteristics. Error analysis can thus result in (*a*) more rapid identification of patterns of errors, and (*b*) effective help. To record a child's reading errors requires the use of a shorthand such as that shown in Table 3. An arrangement of the IRI extract combined with the error categories in columns, as in Table 4, makes for easy recording and assignment of reading level of material.

Goodman (in Smith 1973) presents a valuable overview of current work in the field of error analysis. Goodman considers that reading errors are 'miscues' and should not be responded to negatively by labelling them 'wrong'. The taxonomy that he presents for the analysis of a child's oral miscues comprises twenty-

Table 3
Coding for recording error types

Sentence to be read	Error category	Method of recording error	Example
Which is the way to the house on the hill?	Substitution	Underline the word misread and write in word substituted	'home' Which is the way to the house on the hill?
	No response	If the child *waits* to be prompted or asks for a word, underline with a dashed line	Which is the way to the house on the hill?
	Addition	Use caret mark and write down word or part-word added	'go to' Which is the way to the house on the hill?
	Omission*	Where words are omitted, circle them	Which is the way to the (house) on the hill?
	Self-correction	Where errors are self-corrected, record by using initials 'S.C.' over the words	S.C. Which is the way to the house on the hill?
	Repetition	Record word/s repeated by putting 'R' over appropriate section.	R Which is the way to the house on the hill?
	Mispronunciations	Indicate where stress is placed	
	Ignores punctuation	Circle punctuation ignored	Which is the way to the house on the hill(?) . . . . . .
	Reversals	This is a form of substitution, but may be of diagnostic significance if part of a regular pattern	'no' Which is the way to the house on the hill?

* Child does not wait for help.

Table 4

IRI and error analysis

Extracts from graded material forming basis of IRI	Error Categories								
	Substitution	No Response	Addition	Omission (words)	Self-Correction	Repetition	Mispronunciation	Ignores Punctuation	Reversals
'Come with me', said Peter to Mary.									
asked 'Where to?' she <u>replied</u>.	1								
our 'Over to the canal to get some frogspawn for ⟨ school ⟨.⟩'			1					1	
'I know (where) there is a lot and we can (easily) get it.'				2					
saw Mary <u>was</u> uneasy. 'The canal is (dangerous),' she replied. 'My mother has	1*			1					1*
told me not [to] go near it.'									

50 words to here

	Accuracy	*Comprehension*
(a) Errors:	7 errors	2/10 questions incorrect
(b) % Correct:	86% correct	80% correct
(c) Reading Level:	Instructional	Instructional level

* Refers to same error, but does *not* increase total number of errors made.

Comment: Both accuracy and comprehension indicate Instructional level.
Reads rapidly and tends to omit words as a consequence.
If similar pattern of errors occurs in other samples, will give help with extending sight vocabulary of certain words using flash-cards. Tape child's reading and get him to identify his own omissions.

eight categories. This type of error analysis is extremely time consuming although it is claimed that it has considerable potential in suggesting diagnostic procedures in both classroom and clinic.

The analysis of children's oral reading errors, especially in the early stages of reading acquisition, can be of considerable importance to the teacher. However, it is necessary that the approach be kept in perspective. It can be argued that errors of oral reading are unimportant provided that the child grasps the meaning of what he reads.

References

CHRISTENSON, A. (1969) 'Oral reading errors in intermediate grade children at their independent, instructional, and frustration levels.' In FIGUREL, J. A. (Ed.) *Reading and Realism* I.R.A. Proceedings, **13** (1).

JOHNSON, M. S. and KRESS, R. A. (1972) 'Why informal reading inventories?' In MELNIK, A. and MERRITT, J. (Eds.) *The Reading Curriculum* London: Hodder and Stoughton Educational.

MCCRACKEN, R. A. (1971) 'The Informal Reading Inventory as a Means of Improving Instruction.' In DECHANT, E. (Ed.) *Detection and Correction of Reading Difficulties* New York: Appleton-Century-Crofts.

SMITH, F. (1973) *Psycholinguistics and Reading* New York: Holt, Rinehart and Winston.

VALMONT, W. J. (1972) 'Creating questions for informal reading inventories.' In MELNIK, A. and MERRIT, J. (Eds.) *The Reading Curriculum* London: Hodder and Stoughton Educational.

Further reading

BETTS, E. A. (1957) *Foundations of Reading Instruction* New York: American Book Co.

JOHNSON, M. S. and KRESS, R. A. (1971) 'Individual Reading Inventories.' In DECHANT, E. (Ed.) *Detection and Correction of Reading Difficulties* New York: Appleton-Century-Crofts.

STRANG, R. (1972) 'Informal Reading Inventories.' In MELNIK, A. and MERRITT, J. (Eds.) *The Reading Curriculum* London: Hodder and Stoughton Educational.

Section II

Test Information

4 Reading Test Information and Comments

This chapter is divided into four parts, as follows:

1. Some screening and diagnostic tests of physical aspects of children's readiness for reading. These include tests of hearing, sight, visual-motor co-ordination, language, articulation and vocabulary;
2. Recognised tests of Reading-Readiness, usually with a diagnostic orientation;
3. Reading tests and batteries of tests, attainment and diagnostic; and
4. Attitude to reading scales.

Within each part, tests are presented alphabetically, British produced tests coming first, and tests produced in other countries next.

For each test the following pieces of information are given wherever possible:

(a) Test reference number (hereafter TRN) keyed to an alphabetic index of the tests presented, given on pages 45 to 47;
(b) Name of the test or battery of tests;
(c) Author;
(d) Country of origin of the test;
(e) Publisher;
(f) Year or years of publication;
(g) Type of test plus test user classification as employed by the NFER;
(h) Number and designation of parallel forms;
(i) Chronological age range of subjects for whom the test is intended. The convention used is that, for example, the range of from 5 years 1 month to 6 years 11 months is given as 5 : 1 to 6 : 11;
(j) Skills or other aspects of behaviour tested or rated;
(k) Average administration time and also whether or not the test is a timed one;
(l) Brief description of the test and comments on it. The comments given are not intended to provide a detailed critical evaluation, but draw attention to points the writer considers important.

Though this is not intended as an exhaustive survey of reading tests, the writer has included what he thinks are the most important reading tests currently in use in Great Britain. In general, the tremendous resources that have been devoted to the construction of reading tests in the USA in particular means that many of their instruments are superior to some of those produced in the UK. To give the reader an indication of the range of reading tests produced in other English-speaking countries, a limited number of non-British tests with interesting characteristics is described.

Finding the appropriate test

Tables 5 and 6 on pages 43 and 44, can be used to locate information in the book concerning tests suitable for a given purpose with a given age group of pupils. The numbers given in these two tables relate to the Index of Tests, on pages 45-47. The Index of Tests is arranged alphabetically and, in addition, serially numbered from 1 to 91. These numbers are the Test Reference Numbers (TRNs).

Table 5 contains the TRNs of instruments of use mainly at the descriptive level of interpretation. Table 6 gives the TRNs of instruments having a diagnostic orientation.

To identify the instruments most likely to be of use to her, the teacher needs to decide:

(a) the level of interpretation in which she is mainly interested, i.e. descriptive (Table 5) or diagnostic (Table 6);
(b) the goal with which she is concerned; i.e. attainments or attitudes;
(c) the source of information that she wishes to utilise, i.e. informal, standardised or criterion-referenced; and
(d) the age level with which she is concerned.

By looking at the appropriate cell in either Table 5 or 6, the Test Reference Numbers of some potentially appropriate instruments will be found. By consulting the Index of Tests, the name of the test or other instrument and its country of origin can readily be ascertained. It is then possible to turn to the appropriate part of Chapter 4 and locate information on the instrument.

For example, the teacher might have decided that she is interested in the diagnostic level of interpretation in relation to reading attainment, using information from a standardised test. Such decisions will direct her attention to Table 6 and to the column headed 'Standardised' under the goal of 'Attainments'. If the age level with which she is concerned is, say, thirteen to fourteen years, TRN 12 might be of interest. Turning to the Index of Tests, it will be seen that the test referred to is the California Phonics Survey. This test is an American one and details of it can be found on page 112.

If this particular test is not suitable, the other tests indicated in the pertinent section of Table 6 can readily be located and considered. Alternatively, the teacher can look at the range of tests in the appropriate parts of Chapter 4.

Some blank test information sheets are printed on pages 139 to 144 for readers to record details of further reading tests.

Table 5

Tests and assessment procedures classified by age level according to goals (attainments or attitudes), source of information (informal, standardised, criterion-referenced) and level of interpretation (descriptive*)
(*The numbers refer to those given as Test Reference Numbers in the Index of Tests, pp. 45 to 47*)

Source of information	Goals					
	Attainments			Attitudes		
	Informal	Standardised	Criterion-referenced	Informal	Standardised	Criterion-referenced
Pre-reading level	77	13, 25, 30, 54, 56, 74, 83	34, 36, 51, 79	77		
Infant	44, 77	6, 10, 11, 13, 15, 21, 25, 30, 37, 40, 42, 45, 50, 54, 55, 56, 74, 76, 78, 79, 83, 85, 86, 89, 91	7, 8, 34, 36, 44, 47a, 51, 79, 89	44, 77	33	44
Junior	44, 77	5, 6, 10, 11, 15, 21, 22, 23, 24, 25, 27, 28, 29, 30, 37, 38, 39, 40, 42, 46, 47, 48, 50, 55, 57, 58, 59, 60, 61, 64, 69, 70, 75, 76, 76a, 78, 78a, 79, 86, 87, 89, 91	7, 8, 44, 47a, 52, 70, 79, 89	44, 77	19, 33, 88	44
Secondary	44, 71	2, 6, 9, 10, 11, 15, 21, 24, 25, 27, 28, 30, 37, 38, 40, 46, 49, 50, 55, 61, 62, 64, 65, 69, 70, 73, 76, 76a, 78a, 79, 86, 87, 89	7, 8, 44, 47a, 70, 79, 89, 90	44, 71	32	44
Tertiary	44, 71	9, 14, 25, 30, 37, 38, 55, 65, 72, 73, 76a, 89	44, 89, 90	44, 71	32	44

* N.B. The above classification is a tentative and simplified one indicating the major emphasis of the tests.

Table 6

Tests and assessment procedures classified by age level according to goals (attainments or attitudes), source of information (informal, standardised, criterion-referenced) and level of interpretation (diagnostic*)
(*The numbers refer to those given as Test Reference Numbers in the Index of Tests, pp. 45 to 47*)

Source of information	Goals					
	Attainments			Attitudes		
	Informal	Standardised	Criterion-referenced	Informal	Standardised	Criterion-referenced
Pre-reading	77	13, 16, 20, 26, 30, 31, 41, 43, 54, 56, 74, 83, 84	3a, 36, 67, 68, 79, 89	77		
Infant	44, 77	4, 13, 16, 18, 20, 21, 26, 30, 31, 35, 41, 43, 45, 54, 56, 74, 76, 81, 83, 84, 85, 89, 91	1, 3, 3a, 7, 8, 20, 36, 44, 47a, 51, 52, 63, 66, 67, 68, 79, 82, 89	44, 77	33	44
Junior	44, 77	4, 16, 18, 20, 21, 22, 23, 24, 26, 29, 35, 38, 43, 46, 53, 64, 69, 75a, 76, 78a, 80, 81, 84, 87, 89, 91	1, 3, 3a, 7, 8, 17, 20, 44, 47a, 52, 63, 66, 67a, 79, 82, 89	44, 77	33	44, 84
Secondary	44, 71	12, 16, 18, 21, 24, 35, 38, 46, 64, 65, 69, 73, 76, 76a, 78a, 80, 84, 87, 89	1, 7, 8, 44, 47a, 66, 67a, 73, 79, 82, 89, 90	44, 71		44, 84
Tertiary	44, 71	12, 16, 38, 65, 73, 76a, 84, 89	1, 44, 73, 82, 89, 90	44, 71		44, 84

* N.B. The above classification is a tentative and simplified one indicating the major emphasis of the tests.

Index of Tests

Country of origin is shown in brackets as follows:

(A) = Australia
(B) = Britain
(C) = Canada
(E) = Eire
(J) = Japan
(NZ) = New Zealand
(USA) = United States of America

* TRN—Test Reference Number as classified in Tables 5 and 6, pp. 43 and 44.

* See chapter 3.

1 Some screening and diagnostic tests of physical aspects of children's readiness for reading

Within the UK educational system, the majority of children have started to read by the age of about six years. However, there will be a considerable number of slow-learning children who will not have begun. These children are usually recognised by the teacher and a programme of pre-reading activities geared to their individual needs is devised. Amongst this group of children apparently requiring a further period of pre-reading experience, there can be hidden a number of children who are unable to read not because of dullness, but because of other reasons which may have been overlooked.

For example, although not deaf in the sense that his difficulties are clear to all, a child can suffer from impaired hearing. He may be failing to hear (unknowingly and unknown) certain parts of spoken language. A mild degree of high-frequency deafness would be one example of such a difficulty. The child's ability to discriminate between sounds or between certain similarly sounding spoken words will be diminished and some of his misunderstandings may be interpreted as typical of dullness when this may not be the case. The child's ability to match normally important sound discriminations to their visual presentation will also be adversely affected, e.g. matching sounds of letters or words to their visual representation. Hence reading will be a difficult task and the likelihood of failure to master necessary skills increased.

Similarly, the child with weakness of visual perception may be unable to discriminate certain written symbols such as letters and words and match these to their sounded or spoken equivalents.

His failure to do so can in certain circumstances be wrongly attributed to dullness.

Both of the above paragraphs emphasise the importance of the child being able to receive the sensory stimulation on which he is to operate, and also to establish the equivalence of signs or symbols in more than one sense modality. There are many other physical disabilities frequently associated with difficulties in reading, for example, poor speech and articulation, and clumsiness in other aspects of coordination such as eye-hand. Such conditions may also mislead the teacher into thinking that a child's need for more pre-reading activities is attributable to general immaturity or dullness, rather than to a specific disability which might be alleviated. The situation is made doubly difficult for the teacher because the relationships previously mentioned between certain physical disabilities and immature reading skill attainments are not necessarily causal ones. A child with poor vision may or may not read adequately. Nevertheless, the *possibility* that a physical disability is responsible for a child's slow acquisition of reading skills should always be considered. If such a physical disability is found to exist, the implications for the child's programme of reading activities may be profound.

If a teacher suspects that a child's hearing, sight, coordination or articulation is in some way defective, the Community Physician (Child Health)* will on request and with the parents' permission, carry out the necessary investigations. These may require diagnosis and treatment by audiologists, physiotherapists or speech-

* Known as the School Health Service Medical Officer before the 1974 reorganisation of the Health Services.

therapists concurrently with the child's educational programme if the effects of any disability on the acquisition of reading or any other skill are to be minimised.

In the majority or cases the regular screening surveys carried out by the Community Physician (Child Health) will identify children with the types of defect indicated above. However, children have been known to be absent at the times of such medical examinations or otherwise to have slipped through the net. The pressures of work on the Service are such that all children missing medical examinations are not necessarily followed up. In such a situation it is of value for the teacher to be aware of some relatively simple screening tests of hearing, vision and co-ordination.

Tests of articulation and vocabulary have been included in this section. Although both of these aspects of language development underpin reading competencies, neither involves decoding a printed alphabet.

Pre-reading materials as screening tests
The majority of pre-reading material contains games intended to develop the young child's aural and visual discrimination and visual-motor coordination. These can be used as informal screening tests in many instances.

(a) British

TRN	Name of test	Author	Country	Publisher	Year
15	*Crichton Vocabulary Scale*	J. C. Raven	B	H. K. Lewis	1958

Type	No. of forms	C.A. range	Skills tested	Time
Individual, oral	1	4 : 6 to 11 : 0	Oral definition	Untimed

(level P)

Comments: This test was constructed for use with Raven's *Coloured Progressive Matrices,* a non-verbal test of intelligence. The scale consists of two parallel sets of forty words. The words are arranged in order of difficulty and the child's task is to define in his own words the stimulus word presented orally by the tester. The sample on which the norms are based is limited and the standardisation procedure is rather obscure. Satisfactory test-retest reliabilities are reported. These are given as 0·87 and 0·95 at the 6 : 6 and 9 : 6 levels. The correlations with other tests are also reported. The raw scores can be converted to percentiles for each six months of age between 4 : 6 and 11 : 0.

TRN	Name of test	Author	Country	Publisher	Year
25	*English Picture Vocabulary Tests 1-3*	M. A. Brimer and L. M. Dunn	B	Distributed by Educational Evaluation Enterprises, Bristol	1962 (1 & 2) 1970 (3)

Type	No. of forms	C.A. Range	Skills tested	Time
Test 1 Individual, oral	1	3 : 0 to 4 : 11	Listening vocabulary (40 items)	Untimed
	1	5 : 0 to 8 : 11	Listening vocabulary (40 items)	
Test 2 Individual or group, oral	1	7 : 0 to 11 : 11	Listening vocabulary (40 items)	
Test 3 Individual or group, oral	1	11 : 0 to adult	Listening vocabulary (48 items)	

(level A)

Comments: One important characteristic of this series is that they do not require the child to have any reading attainments. The items used to make Tests 1 and 2 are each a page of four pictures plus a spoken word. The child's task is to indicate the picture to which the spoken word refers. Test 1 has a pre-school and an infant age version. It is an individual test whereas Tests 2 and 3 can be given either individually or to a group. The format of Test 3 presents sixteen items on each of three pages of a printed record sheet. These tests are an adaptation of the American *Peabody Picture Vocabulary Test*. However, the authors have completely reconstructed the test for use with English children. For Tests 1 and 2, the standardisation procedure was carried out on samples of 3240 and 5084 Wiltshire children selected so as to ensure close agreement with national characteristics. Interestingly, boys scored consistently higher than girls at every age level tested. This difference is claimed to be due to differences in the functions being tested. Despite this, it is argued that the uses for which the tests are intended do not require that separate norms for boys and girls be prepared. The internal consistency reliabilities of the tests at each age level from 5 : 0 to 8 : 11 are fairly high (Test 1: from 0·87 to 0·89 for each group and 0·92 for the total 5 : 0 to 8 : 11 range; Test 2: 0·88 to 0·93 for each year group and 0·96 for the four-year range.) Content validity seems adequate. Other evidence of validities is sparse and the intercorrelations presented are open to many interpretations. Test 3 in the series was standardised on 8994 subjects, representatively drawn from students and adults engaged in full or part-time education. The internal consistency reliabilities range from 0·88 to 0·94. Test-retest reliabilities are to be published shortly. A 'full range' edition of the above series of tests is now available.

TRN	Name of test	Author	Country	Publisher	Year
34	*Getting Ready for Reading Tests of Hearing*	E. H. Grassam	B	Ginn and Co. Ltd, London	1960

Type	No. of forms	C.A. range	Skills tested	Time
Individual, oral, screening (level A)	1	5 : 0+	1. Auditory acuity 2. Sentence repetition 3. Sound discrimination	Untimed (30′)

Comments: All of these tests can be found in the Teachers' Manual to *Getting Ready for Reading* in the Beacon Reading Series. The first test is referred to as the 'whisper test'. It requires that the tester stands twenty feet from the child in a quiet room and whispers a series of twenty words. The child stands with his side towards the tester, the ear remote from the teacher covered. The child is asked to repeat each word as the tester utters it. This procedure is repeated with the other ear covered and with both ears uncovered. Twenty words selected from a list appropriate to the age of the child and including representative consonant and vowel combinations are presented. Correct repetition of 18/20 of the words is deemed to indicate hearing acuity probably adequate in the typical class situation. As the child in school is not expected to learn from a teacher who uses whispered speech, some workers doubt the validity of such a test. Certainly the control of volume, pitch and intonation is unlikely to be standard. Common sense suggests that such a screening test of auditory acuity should give a good indication of a child's hearing for normal connected speech, as well as for whispered, distinct words. This information can be simply and conveniently obtained by delivering standard lists of words, sentences and nonsense syllables in certain cases. Such tests suffice as screening procedures only. If there is any doubt concerning a child's hearing ability, a full audiometric investigation should be arranged.

The second Grassam test requires that the child repeat a series of test sentences, each of six words spoken aloud by the teacher. Any error in the child's repetition of a sentence represents failure on that sentence. Inability to repeat at least five sentences is claimed to be indicative of a defect of *either* hearing *or* retention. The third test involves the child being asked to say whether two sounds, spoken by the teacher standing behind the child, are alike or different, e.g. b—d; th—sh. A list of twenty-four pairs of sounds is given and unless the pupil can distinguish 14/24 correctly, it is claimed that his auditory discrimination is not good enough for him to learn to read by approaches used with children whose hearing is normal.

Both of the suggested interpretations of the above two further screening tests seem rather too definite to be completely valid. Whilst some evidence supporting the interpretation of the first two tests is referred to, none is mentioned in connection with the third one. The manual gives none of the information concerning standardisation, reliabilities and validities normally expected of tests. However, despite their weaknesses, the tests enable the teacher to carry out a rapid screening of children whose hearing may be suspect. It is important to bear in mind Grassam's stricture that the tests 'do not measure the extent or the cause of a child's hearing deficiency, but they enable the teacher to discover the child whose auditory perception is inadequate. The child should then be referred to a specialist'.

TRN	Name of test	Author	Country	Publisher	Year
55	*Mill Hill Vocabulary Scale*	J. C. Raven	B	H. K. Lewis	1943

Type	No. of forms	C.A. range	Skills tested		Time
Individual and group, oral and written, attainment and diagnostic	1 (Definitions Form)	4 : 6 to 14 : 0 70 : 0 to 85 : 0	1. Word definitions		Untimed (10'-20')
	2 (Form 1 Senior and Junior)	11 : 6 to 60 : 0	1. Word definitions 2. Synonym selection		
(level P)	2 (Form 2 Senior and Junior)	11 : 6 to 60 : 0	1. Synonym selection 2. Word definitions		

Comments: Constructed as a complementary test to the non-verbal Raven's *Standard Progressive Matrices*, this scale consists of two parallel series of forty-four words known as sets A and B. In Form 1 of the scale, children able to read and write are asked to write down the meaning of words in set A and also to select a synonym from six alternatives for each word in set B. This procedure is reversed in Form 2. It is claimed that the oral administration of the scale gives similar results with such children. Children unable to write can be given the Definitions Form of the scale orally.

The standardisation both as individual and group tests for children was carried out on various samples of school children in Colchester, Essex. The test-retest reliabilities presented for the written form of the test seem acceptable, ranging from 0·87 to 0·98 for five age groups. Various groups of adults were tested during 1946 and 1947 and percentile equivalents for raw scores on the scale are presented for them. The major weakness of the scale is that relatively few items cover a vast range of vocabularies.

TRN	Name of test	Author	Country	Publisher	Year
67	*Picture Screening Test of Hearing*	M. Reed	B	Royal National Institute for the Deaf	1960

Type	No. of forms	C.A. range	Skills tested	Time
Individual, oral, screening, criterion-referenced	1	5 : 0+	Aural discrimination	Untimed (10′)

(level A)

Comments: The purpose of this test is to enable the teacher to establish whether or not a child has a slight hearing loss which could affect the child's ability to learn skills such as reading and to give the incorrect impression of being dull. The test is in the form of a spirally bound booklet consisting of eight cards. On each card is a coloured picture of four common objects. The names of the objects on a given card contain the same vowel sound, but different consonants; for example:

MOUSE : OWL : COW : HOUSE

The test depends on the fact that, in hearing impairment, consonants rather than vowels are the first elements of speech to be misheard. Having made certain that the child knows the names of the pictures on a given card, the tester stands *behind* the child to prevent lip-reading and asks the child to point to each object in turn. The child who points to a number of incorrect pictures is probably having difficulty in differentiating between certain sounds. According to the instructions, any child failing on two or more pictures on two or more cards should be referred for a full audiometric examination. No information is given concerning the reliability or validity of this screening test. However, it has the imprimatur of the Royal National Institute for the Deaf.

TRN	Name of test	Author	Country	Publisher	Year
74	*Reynell Developmental Language Scales* (experimental edition)	J. Reynell	B	NFER	1969

Type	No. of forms	C.A. range	Skills tested	Time
Individual, diagnostic	1	0 : 6 to 6 : 0	1. Verbal comprehension scale A (no speech by the child required) 2. Verbal comprehension scale B (adaptation of scale A for severely handicapped children) 3. Expressive language scales: (a) language structure (b) vocabulary (c) content, with emphasis on creative uses of language	Untimed (20')

(level K)

Comments: This test was designed for the assessment of young children's receptive and expressive language abilities. The experimental edition of the test was standardised on not less than twenty-five boys and twenty-five girls at each six months of age from six months to six years inclusive. No children of recent immigrants were included as their language development might be atypical for an English standardisation. Acceptably high internal consistency reliabilities of the sub-scales at various ages are presented together with inter-scale correlations. These reliabilities range from 0·77 to 0·92. Norms are provided in terms of Age Scores, Standard Scores and via graphs for boys and girls separately in each area covered by the scales. It is highly likely that the systematic observation of children's language development built into the test will stimulate ideas concerning ways in which given aspects of language development might be facilitated.

TRN	Name of test	Author	Country	Publisher	Year
76a	*Schools Council Oracy Project: Listening Comprehension Tests*	A. Wilkinson, L. Stratta and P. Dudley	B	Macmillan Educational	1974

Type	No. of forms	C.A. Range	Skills tested	items in batteries			Time*
Individual or group, attainment and diagnostic	3		*Listening comprehension*	A	B	C	
	A	10 : 0 to 11 : 0	i. Test of content	15	12	12	59′
			ii. Test of contextual constraint	15	19	15	
	B	13 : 0 to 14 : 0	iii. Test of phonology	15	18		62′
			iv. Test of register	15	15	17	
(level A)	C	17 : 0 to 18 : 0	v. Test of relationships	15	15	18	78′

Comments: The three batteries are designed to measure subjects' listening comprehension of a variety of tape-recorded spoken materials. Each differs slightly in its composition. A and B each contains all of the above five sub-tests, whereas C does not include a test of phonology. Although in each battery each sub-test focuses on one element of listening comprehension, all the sub-tests are related. The batteries give a normative listening comprehension score indicating relative level of performance over the sub-tests. The profile of sub-test scores can be used for diagnostic purposes although such work is still in its infancy. Additionally, the taped stimulus materials are intended to provide ideas that can be adapted and developed by teachers for interesting language work in schools.

The tests have been standardised on samples of 180, 1152 and 133 pupils for batteries A, B and C respectively. The internal consistency reliabilities of the batteries are 0·777, 0·827 and 0·838. Correlations with measures of intelligence, reading and aspects of personality are reported. The intercorrelations of the sub-tests in each battery are given. Sex differences in scores on the tests are reported. For battery B the large-scale testing enabled standard scores with a mean of 100 and a standard deviation of 15 to be calculated. Batteries A and C are less adequately standardised. The relationships between listening and reading comprehension could be explored by teachers using the above instruments to assess the former in their particular situation. In the authors' opinion, the test materials are seen '. . . as exemplifying features and functions of the spoken language which should be part of the knowledge of every teacher . . .'.

A research report on the Schools Council Oracy Project by the above authors is presented in *The Quality of Listening* published in 1974 by Macmillan Educational.

* It is recommended that each battery be administered in two parts with a 30′ break. Thus the actual times for administration are: Battery A, $1\frac{1}{2}$ hrs; Battery B, $1\frac{3}{4}$ hrs; Battery C, $1\frac{3}{4}$ to 2 hrs.

(b) Others

TRN	Name of test	Author	Country	Publisher	Year
1	*American Optical Pseudoisochromatic Plates*	L. H. Hardy, G. Rand and M. C. Rittler	USA	American Optical Co. (British-American Optical act as agents)	1957

Type	No. of forms	C.A. range	Skills tested	Time
Individual, criterion-referenced, diagnostic	1	5 : 0+	Colour vision	Untimed (8')
(level P)				

Comments: It is claimed that this test is an improvement on the Ishihara Test (see p. 61) as it enables a subject's degree of colour-vision defect to be more reliably quantified. Some evidence of validity is presented in the test manual. If a colour-coded reading scheme is in use, children with certain types of colour-blindness (usually boys) might be unwittingly presented with inappropriate material.

TRN	Name of test	Author	Country	Publisher	Year
4	*Auditory Discrimination Test*	J. M. Wepman	USA	Language Research Associates	1958

Type	No. of forms	C.A. range	Skills tested	Time
Individual, oral, diagnostic	2 (I & II)	5 : 0 to 8 : 0 (approx.)	Auditory discrimination	Untimed (10')
(level A)				

Comments: Wepman considers auditory discrimination to be highly related to the development of speech accuracy and, to a lesser degree, reading attainments. The forty-item test is an easily administered method of assessing the child's ability to distinguish certain fine distinctions between phonemes used in English speech. The child listens while the tester reads pairs of words from a given list. The child's task is to indicate either verbally or otherwise whether the words sound the same or different. When poor discrimination has been identified, remedial work can be planned. The standardisation of the test was initially on 533 unselected six to eight-year-old children. Test-retest reliability is high (0·91) and evidence of validities is presented. The tester is asked to read the words *facing* the child. This could lead to a child using visual cues, i.e. lip-reading, rather than being concerned with auditory discriminations. Despite this reservation, the test is an accurate and easy to administer measure of auditory discrimination.

TRN	Name of test		Author		Country	Publisher		Year
26	*Frostig Developmental Test of Visual Perception*		M. Frostig		USA	Consulting Psychologists Press (NFER act as agents)		1963

Type	No. of forms	C.A. range	Skills tested	Time
Individual, small group, diagnostic	1	3 : 0 to 10 : 0	1. Eye-motor coordination	30'-45'
			2. Figure-ground discrimination	
			3. Constancy of shape	
			4. Position in space	
(level P)			5. Spatial relationships	

Comments: This test claims to measure five important but relatively unrelated aspects of visual perception. Normative information is based on 2116 normal children aged between four and eight years. This is reported in three-monthly chronological age intervals. The results are presented in profile form. The test-retest reliabilities of some of the sub-tests are well below 0·5. The theoretical basis of this test has been vigorously attacked and the relative independence of the sub-tests questioned by researchers. However, if visual perception is one component of reading ability, this test does begin to look closely at children's performances in an interesting way. Provided one exercises appropriate caution in interpreting the profiles for individuals, the test can give indications of children's strengths and weaknesses.

The training programme that Frostig has produced claims to improve children's visual perception. Whether the training programme is effective *because* it is similar to the various tests on the *Developmental Test of Visual Perception*, is currently being investigated. Earlier claims that, after identification of visual-perceptual weaknesses and strengths followed by appropriate training on the Frostig Programme, improvement in visual-perceptual *and* reading attainments occurred, have not been substantiated as yet.

TRN	Name of test	Author	Country	Publisher	Year
36	*Goldman-Fristoe Test of Articulation*	R. Goldman and M. Fristoe	USA	American Guidance Service, Inc.	1969

Type	No. of forms	C.A. range	Skills tested	Time
Individual, criterion-referenced (levels A and K)	1	2 : 0+	1. Sounds in words 2. Sounds in sentences 3. Stimulability (the ability to produce a previously misarticulated phoneme when given maximum cues, both visual and oral)	Untimed (10')

Comments: Errors in articulation are frequently found in groups of children with reading difficulties. This test enables a systematic assessment to be made of an individual's ability to articulate consonant sounds. If the ability to articulate correctly or not is to be assessed, a teacher could use the test. If each sound production is to be further judged for type of error, one needs to have had appropriate advanced training.

The materials are colourful and interesting to children. The test-retest and inter-rater reliabilities are acceptably high, though not expressed in conventional terms. The test is very well compiled and convenient to use.

TRN	Name of test	Author	Country	Publisher	Year
43	*Illinois Test of Psycholinguistic Abilities* (revised edition)	S. A. Kirk, J. McCarthy and W. Kirk	USA	University of Illinois Press (NFER act as agents)	1968

Type	No. of forms	C.A. range	Skills tested		Time
Individual, diagnostic	1	2 : 4 to 10 : 3	1. Auditory reception 2. Visual reception 3. Auditory association 4. Visual association 5. Verbal expression 6. Manual expression 7. Grammatic closure * Supplementary tests	8. Visual closure (timed) 9. Auditory sequential memory 10. Visual sequential memory 11. Auditory closure* 12. Sound blending*	45′ approx.
(level P)					

Comments: This test is designed to allow an analysis of children's psycholinguistic abilities. The three dimensions deemed important are: (a) Channels of communication (auditory-vocal; visual-motor), (b) Processes (reception; organisation; expression), and (c) Levels of organisation or complexity (automatic level; representational level). Results can be expressed as a Composite Psycholinguistic Age, an estimated Binet mental age and IQ, and as scaled scores for each of the sub-tests. This allows profile interpretation. The standardisation is satisfactory but was restricted to 'children of average intelligence, school achievement, and socio-economic status and of intact motor and sensory development'. The tests are generally acceptably reliable. The evidence on validities is extensive, but is not included in the test manual. The intercorrelations of the sub-tests are also not given, thus making profile interpretation unnecessarily difficult. Kirk and his colleagues have written several monographs, including one on the diagnosis and remediation of psycholinguistic abilities, based on the ITPA.

This is an extremely promising instrument. It is so, largely because the model of language on which it is based ensures that three major dimensions of information processing underlying reading abilities are systematically conceptualised and investigated.

TRN	Name of test	Author	Country	Publisher	Year
82	*Tests for Colour-Blindness*	S. Ishihara	J	Kanehara Shuppan Co. (NFER act as agents)	1971 1970

Type	No. of forms	C.A. range	Skills tested	Time
Individual, diagnostic (level P)	2 (24-plate and 38-plate)	6 : 0+	Ability to perceive colours and discriminate between colours	Untimed (10')

Comments: If a child (usually a boy) suffers from one of the many forms of colour-blindness, it is possible that certain reading schemes using colour codes may confuse rather than assist the child to learn the discriminations apparent to children whose colour vision is normal. In such a case, a teacher may mistakenly assume that a child with a colour-vision deficiency is a slow-learner of the colour-coded material.

The above test can be used with children who know their number names or can match cards containing written numbers. Although the above dates of publication are those of the most recent editions of the test, it has been in use for many years. The norms are elementary and details of standardisation are not given. The test can perhaps be considered as a mastery type test in which failure to cope with a prescribed number of items has important implications concerning the use of colour-coded reading schemes with a child.

TRN	Name of test	Author	Country	Publisher	Year
84	*Visual Motor Gestalt Test*	L. Bender	USA	American Orthopsychiatric Association (NFER act as agents)	1946

Type	No. of forms	C.A. range	Skills tested	Time
Individual, diagnostic (level K)	1	4 : 0 to 11 : 0 (and adults)	Used *clinically* as: 1. Test of visual motor-gestalt maturation 2. To explore retardation, regression, loss of function 3. To explore personality deviations where there are regressive phenomena	Untimed (15′)

Comments: In this test the subject is asked to reproduce a series of eight designs. The responses are interpreted in terms of Gestalt laws of perception and organisation.

The test manual gives nothing in the way of conventional psychometric information.

Studies of children and adults are to be found in Research Monograph Number 3 of the American Orthopsychiatric Association (1938) by Bender. Since then a wide variety of scoring systems have been devised. Those by Koppitz (1964) and by Pascal and Suttell (1950) attempt to quantify children's and adults' responses respectively.* The theoretical basis of the test is complex and the test is only available to psychologists of equivalent training and experience to qualify for Associate Membership of the British Psychological Society.

* Koppitz, E. M. (1964) *The Bender Gestalt Test for Young Children* New York: Grune and Stratton.

Pascal, G. R. and Suttell, B. J. (1950) *The Bender-Gestalt Test: Its Quantification and Validity for Adults* New York: Grune and Stratton.

TRN 85	Name of test *Vocabulary Survey Test*		Author M. Monroe, J. C. Manning and J. M. Wepman	Country USA	Publisher Scott, Foresman & Co.	Year 1971

Type Group, attainment and diagnostic (level A)	No. of forms 2 (A & B)	C.A. range 5 : 0 to 7 : 0	Skills tested Comprehension of oral vocabulary 1. Nouns, mathematical terms 2. Place relationship terms, verbs, adjectives, pronouns, mathematical concepts	Time Untimed (2 sessions)

Comments: This test is designed to assess aspects of oral vocabulary. In both parts, the teacher dictates a word or a phrase and the child selects one of four picture options.

The standardisation sample is clearly described, but is hardly a typical one. Raw scores can be converted to standard scores and percentiles. The split-half reliability of the test is 0·93. The manual is very helpful concerning the interpretation of, and possible action based on, the children's responses.

2 Recognised tests of reading readiness

(a) British

TRN	Name of test	Author	Country	Publisher	Year
83	*Thackray Reading Readiness Profiles*	D. V. Thackray and L. E. Thackray	B	Hodder and Stoughton Educational	1974

Type	No. of forms	C.A. range	Skills tested	Time
Group, diagnostic	1	4 : 8 to 5 : 8 (approx.)	1. Vocabulary and concept development	20′
			2. Auditory discrimination	20′
			3. Visual discrimination	20′
(level A)			4. General ability	10′

Comments: Those who have read Dr Thackray's book *Readiness for Reading* (1971), London, Chapman, will realise that he has made a long and intensive study of this area. The Thackrays have chosen to carry out pioneer work in an area which has previously been largely American-dominated. The profiles are the first reading-readiness test to be constructed in the UK. It is primarily intended for use with admission class pupils. If considered as a content criterion-referenced test, it could probably be used to some advantage with slightly older children. The aims of the test are to provide quick, reliable and valid measures of what the Thackrays consider the most vital reading-readiness skills. It comes in the form of an attractively presented sixteen-page individual booklet. The test has been standardised on 5500 children aged from 4 : 8 to 5 : 8 drawn from 350 schools in urban and rural areas of Great Britain and Northern Ireland. The split-half reliabilities of the three reading-readiness scales are 0·80, 0·81, and 0·90 respectively. High content validity is claimed and evidence of acceptable predictive validities of the first three scales is given. The intercorrelations of the four scales are given. In addition, the manual contains information on the interpretation of the individual scales plus suggestions for develop-

ing reading-readiness skills in the areas of Language Development, Auditory Discrimination and Visual Discrimination.

The use of the Harris* revision of the Goodenough 'Draw-a-man' Test as a measure of general ability might be considered suspect by some teachers. The norms used for this scale are American. Perhaps of more concern, and despite the caveat entered, the guidance on the clinical interpretation of children's drawings given on page 22 of the manual suggests implications that require important qualification if unjustified overinterpretation is not to occur. Further research on the predictive validity of the profiles is in hand.

It should not be thought that there are no other British tests of reading-readiness skills available. The Standard Reading Tests Battery contains several criterion-referenced diagnostic tests. However, as yet we have no other British normative standardised objective test of reading readiness.

* Harris, D. B. (1963) *Children's drawings as measures of intellectual maturity. A revision and extension of the Goodenough Draw-a-Man Test* New York: Harcourt, Brace and World.

(b) Others

TRN	Name of test	Author	Country	Publisher	Year
13	*Clymer-Barrett Pre-Reading Battery*	T. Clymer and T. C. Barrett	USA	Personnel Press, Inc.	1967

Type	No. of forms	C.A. range	Skills tested	Time
Group or individual, attainment and diagnostic	2 (A & B)	5 : 0 to 6 : 0	*Visual discrimination* 1. Recognition of letters (35 items) 2. Matching words (20 items) *Auditory discrimination* 3. Beginning sounds in words (20 items) 4. Ending sounds in words (20 items) *Visual-motor coordination* 5. Shape completion (20 items) 6. Copy-a-sentence (1 sentence; 7 words; 27 letters) 7. Pre-reading rating scale: (*a*) facility in oral language (*b*) concept and vocabulary development (*c*) skills in critical thinking (*d*) social skills (*e*) emotional development (*f*) attitude towards and interest in reading (*g*) work habits	Short Form 30' Long (Diagnostic) Form (3 × 30' sessions)
(level P)				

Comments: The purpose of this battery is to provide teachers with information that will serve as a basis for matching instruction in pre-reading and early reading skills to the child's individual pattern of skills. The Short Form administration employs only sub-tests 1 and 3 and gives a single score useful for screening and placement. The Long Form gives three diagnostic sub-scores and battery total. Information on the standardisation is rather vague. Reliabilities of sub-tests, intercorrelations and validities are reported. The manual is very helpful in interpreting the scores, but does not give much guidance as to activities likely to facilitate improvement of undeveloped or weak skills.

This battery is at least equal to the *Metropolitan Readiness Tests* in its ability to predict reading success on the *Gates-MacGinitie Vocabulary and Comprehension Reading Tests* for children in grade 1, from a particular American population. The two sub-tests that most accurately predict reading success as defined are numbers 1 and 3.

E

TRN	Name of test	Author	Country	Publisher	Year
31	*Gates-MacGinitie Reading Tests: Readiness Skills*	A. I. Gates and W. H. MacGinitie	USA	Teachers College Press, New York	1939 to 1968

Type	No. of forms	C.A. range	Skills tested	Time
Group, diagnostic	1	5 : 0 to 6 : 0	1. Listening comprehension 2. Auditory discrimination 3. Visual discrimination 4. Following directions 5. Letter recognition 6. Visual-motor coordination 7. Auditory blending 8. Word recognition 9. Total score	4 × 30′ sessions

(level A)

Comments: The child's scores on this test can be presented in a profile showing weaknesses and strengths in the areas tested. The Word Recognition sub-test is intended to help in the rapid identification of those children who have acquired some reading attainments. This score is *not* included in the total weighted score.

The test was standardised on a nationally representative sample. The reliabilities and validities presented in the Technical Supplement to the manual are satisfactory. Caution in interpreting differences between sub-test scores is emphasised. Raw scores can be converted to stanine scores and to percentiles. The scores from the sub-tests have been weighted so as to give the best prediction of later reading achievement. The total weighted scores of a group can be compared in terms of normalised standard scores called 'Readiness Standard Scores' and in 'Readiness Percentile Scores'.

The manual to the test gives helpful advice in interpreting the scores obtained.

TRN	Name of test		Author		Country	Publisher		Year
41	*Harrison-Stroud Reading Readiness Profiles*		M. L. Harrison and J. B. Stroud		USA	Houghton Mifflin Co. (NFER act as agents)		1949 to 1956

Type	No. of forms	C.A. range	Skills tested	Time
Individual in part, but sections can be administered as a group test; diagnostic

(level P) | 1 | 5 : 0 to 6 : 0 | 1. Using symbols
2. Making visual discriminations (two parts)
3. Using context clues
4. Auditory discriminations
5. Using context and auditory clues
6. Giving the names of letters | Untimed |

Comments: The children's materials in this test are very attractively prepared. The only skills the child requires in order to cope with the first five tests is to be able, on instruction, to underline either a picture or a word or to draw a line joining a word to a picture. The sixth test is of naming letters and is almost entirely dependent on specific teaching, whether by parents or teacher. In this respect sub-test 6 differs from the other tests.

The results are summarised for each child in a profile giving a child's percentile rank for each of the tests. The authors discuss five charac-teristic profiles and indicate the type of programmes appropriate to children with such profiles. Typically, a profile presentation leaves little doubt in the mind of the observer as to a child's relative weaknesses and strengths in the skills tested. Unfortunately, no mention is made in the manual of the reliabilities of the tests or their intercorrelations. Yet such considerations are central if one is to interpret the differences between scores on different sub-tests. Whether the tests are satisfactorily valid is also open to some doubt. Despite such strictures, these tests have been found to be of value by many teachers.

TRN	Name of test	Author	Country	Publisher	Year
45	*Initial Survey Test*	M. Monroe, J. C. Manning, J. M. Wepman and E. G. Gibb	USA	Scott, Foresman & Co.	1972

Type	No. of forms	C.A. range	Skills tested	Time
Group, attainment and diagnostic	2 (A & B)	6 : 0 to 7 : 0	1. Language meanings (20 items)	Untimed
			2. Auditory ability (25 items)	(4 sessions)
			3. Visual ability (21 items)	
			4. Letter recognition (44 items)	
			5. Sound-letter relationships (10 items)	
(level A)			6. Mathematics (15 items)	

Comments: The aim of the test is to help teachers assess each pupil's ability to use the skills that are important to success in beginning primary school learning, with particular emphasis on reading and number. The first five sub-tests were originally published in 1970 as the *Initial Reading Survey Test*. Raw scores can be converted to standard scores and percentiles. Standardisation is clearly described. The test's odd-even (internal consistency) coefficient of reliability is 0·96. Sub-test reliabilities and intercorrelations are not given. No evidence of validities is presented. The manual gives clear help on the interpretation and use of the results.

TRN	Name of test	Author	Country	Publisher	Year
54	*Metropolitan Readiness Tests*	G. H. Hildreth, N. L. Griffiths and M. E. McGauvran	USA	Harcourt, Brace and World, Inc. (NFER act as agents)	1933 to 1966

Type	No. of forms	C.A. range	Skills tested	Time
Group, diagnostic (level R)	2 (R & S)	5 : 0 to 6 : 0	1. Word meaning 2. Listening 3. Matching 4. Alphabet 5. Numbers 6. Copying 7. Draw-a-man (optional)	Untimed (3 sessions)

Comments: This test has been used extensively since its first appearance. It has also undergone successive improvements as a result of its use. From the technical point of view this test is one of the better ones available. The manual contains clear instructions for administering and scoring, and stresses the care needed in the interpretation of a sub-test score for an individual. This is a counsel of caution to be welcomed. This test has produced evidence of being a valid predictor of children's later reading attainments. As such, it is potentially of value to the teacher hoping to maximise the chances of children making satisfactory reading progress.

TRN	Name of test	Author	Country	Publisher	Year
56	*Murphy-Durrell Reading Readiness Analysis*	H. A. Murphy and D. D. Durrell	USA	Harcourt, Brace and World, Inc.	1965

Type	No. of forms	C.A. range	Skills tested	Time
Group and individual, attainment and diagnostic	1	6:0 to 6:11	1. Phoneme identification test (24 items)	Untimed
			2. Letter names test, upper and lower case letters (52 items)	Untimed
(level A)			3. Learning rate test (18 items)	Timed

Comments: This instrument is primarily intended to measure aspects of reading readiness that will help the teacher in grouping entrants to schools for reading instruction. The test was standardised on 12 231 grade 1 pupils from sixty-five school systems in twelve states of the USA. Scores can be converted to percentiles, stanines and quartile groupings. The internal consistency reliabilities for the sub-tests are high, and the extent to which they predict later reading attainment is acceptable. The inter sub-test correlations are sufficiently low to suggest that differentially important components of pre-reading skills are being tested.

TRN 68	Name of test *Pre-reading Assessment Kit*	Author Ontario Institute for Studies in Education	Country C	Publisher California Test Bureau/McGraw-Hill Ryeson Ltd, for Ontario Institute for Studies in Education	Year 1972

Type Group and individual, diagnostic, criterion-referenced	No. of forms See Skills tested	C.A. range 5 : 0 to 6 : 0	Skills tested	6 y.o. Difficulty Level			Time Untimed (about 10′ per test)
				Easy 65%-85%	*Moderate* 40%-65%	*Hard* 25%-40%	
			Listening Unit				
			Rhyming 1	X			
			Rhyming 2	X			
			Beginning sounds		X	X	
			Ending sounds		X	X	
			Symbol Perception Unit				
			Visual discrimination 1	X			
			Visual discrimination 2	X			
			Recognition of letters		X		
			Recognition of words			X	
			Experience Vocabulary Unit				
			Experience vocabulary	X	X		
			Comprehension Unit				
			Classification	X	X		
			Emotional response	X	X		
(level A)			Cause-effect and prediction	X	X		

Comments: This battery was developed by a committee of teachers and members of the Ontario Institute for Studies in Education. The tests are intended to provide diagnostic indications of the specific skills, pertinent to reading, that the child has or has not acquired. The sub-tests are relatively short yet reasonably reliable. The correlations between the sub-tests are sufficiently low to suggest that relatively distinct abilities are being tested. The predictive validity of the instrument appears satisfactory. Suggestions for interpreting the results and for remedial activities are made in the handbook. This test has many possibilities, but its administration, scoring and interpretation is likely to be rather time-consuming if used with classes of children rather than with individuals.

3 Reading tests: attainment and diagnostic

(a) *British*

TRN	Name of test	Author	Country	Publisher	Year
2	*APU Vocabulary Test*	S. J. Close	B	Hodder and Stoughton Educational	1976

Type	No. of forms	C.A. range	Skills tested		Time
Group attainment	1	11 : 0 to 18 : 0	Vocabulary		15′

(level A)

Comments: This 75-item test is designed to assess secondary school children's understanding of currently used vocabulary. The items take the form of synonym selection from a multiple-choice array, for example:

stimulus word	options
CHAIR	poor step seat thick mat

The test is being standardised on a sample of 5000 subjects on which up-to-date norms will be provided.

TRN	Name of test	Author	Country	Publisher	Year
3	*Assessment of Reading Ability*	D. Labon	B	West Sussex County Council (Education Committee Psychological Service)	1972

Type	No. of forms	C.A. range	Skills tested	Time
Individual, diagnostic, keyed to attainment criteria	1	5 : 0 to 11 : 0	1. Schonell Word Recognition Test	Untimed (30')
	1		2. Visual discrimination—Letter Shapes Test	
	1		3. Auditory discrimination—Word Pairs Test	
	1		4. Knowledge of letter sounds	
	1		5. 'Odd Man Out' (initial and final sounds)	
	1		6. Word Building Test	
(level A)	2		7. Letter Sounds Test	

Comments: The above battery of tests has been devised by psychologists and remedial teachers for use with primary school children having reading difficulties. The tests' results are related via a branching 'decision point' programme to a guide suggesting remedial teaching activities likely to improve any weakness diagnosed. The idea is a most helpful one and the author is to be congratulated on his work.

In terms of conventional standardisation procedures and technical information on test reliabilities, validities and intercorrelations, little evidence is presented for the tests devised. This appears to be because the areas sampled are assumed to be used as 'mastery' tests. Thus to become competent readers all children need to master the skills tested at given levels. There is also the intention of not frightening any potential users by presenting psychometric information.

TRN	Name of test	Author	Country	Publisher	Year
3a	*Aston Index* (experimental edition)	M. Newton, C. Ratcliff, G. Scott and M. Thomson	B	The University of Aston in Birmingham	1974

Type	No. of forms	C.A. range	Skills tested	Time
Individual, diagnostic, potentially criterion-referenced	(3) I	5 : 6	*General underlying ability* 1. Picture recognition 3. Goodenough Draw-a-Man Test 2. Vocabulary 4. Copying geometrical designs *Family history* 1. Laterality 3. Knowledge of left and right 2. Birth history 4. General background factors *Performance items* 1. Write or copy name three times 2. Grapheme/phoneme correspondence 3. Visual sequential memory 4. Digits—forward and reverse 5. Sound blending 6. Sound discrimination	Untimed
(level A)	II	7 : 0+	*General underlying ability* 1. Goodenough Draw-a-Man Test 2. Vocabulary 3. Copying geometrical designs *Family history* 1. Laterality 3. Knowledge of left and right 2. Birth history *Performance items* 1. Reading (Schonell Tests) 2. Spelling (Schonell Tests) 3. Grapheme/phoneme correspondence 4. Free writing 5. Graphomotor ability 6. Visual sequential memory 7. Auditory sequential memory 8. Sound blending 9. Sound discrimination	
(level A)				

Aston Index contd.

III

(level K)

Referral to specialist agencies
Further diagnosis may include:
1. Wechsler Intelligence Scale for Children
2. Illinois Test of Psycholinguistic Abilities
3. Neurological tests
4. Sensory mechanism tests

Comments: Dyslexia is a highly controversial concept. The *Aston Index* is designed for both the early diagnosis of 'Dyslexic-type language-difficulties' and as a guide to remedial work.* The authors argue that many children are 'at risk' in our verbally based educational system. Some of these children enter school with a psycho-motor organisation not conducive to the acquisition of reading, spelling and writing mainly because of constitutional characteristics. When these children are faced with the task of mastering the previous language skills, 'the ensuing pattern of presenting symptoms constitutes a "category". The Index attempts to diagnose this category, named by many as "dyslexia"'.

The Index at present comes in three forms. The first is intended for use with the child who has been at school for about six months and in whom low attainments are 'discrepant with apparent "intelligence" and social competence'. The second form is to be administered at 7+ years in cases where discrepant low attainment in reading, writing and spelling is found. The third 'form' is a suggestion that further clinical

diagnosis is necessary and lists instruments that may be used to this end.

Some ten major symptoms are listed, any number of which may or may not be present in the syndrome.

The Index is currently only at an experimental stage (personal communication, September 1974). Some evidence of concurrent validity has been reported and a study of predictive validity is in hand. The problems of interpreting the extremely complex profile of abilities that the tests comprising the Index can provide are tremendous. Interpretation is still largely dependent on the clinical skills and knowledge of the user of the instrument. A great deal of work remains to be done if the Index is to fulfil its authors' intentions.

* Newton, M. and Thomson, M. (1974) *Dyslexia: a guide to teaching* Birmingham: The University of Aston in Birmingham.

Newton, M. and Thomson, M. (1974) 'Towards early diagnosis of dyslexia (Primary reading difficulty).' Paper read at the 11th Annual Study Conference of the UKRA.

TRN	Name of test		Author		Country	Publisher	Year
6	*Ballard Reading Tests*		P. B. Ballard		B	University of London Press	1920

Type	No. of forms	C.A. range	Skills tested	Time
Individual, oral attainment	1	5 : 6 to 16 : 0	One Minute Reading Test (speed of reading simple words)	1′
Group or individual attainment	1	9 : 0 to 14 : 0	Silent Reading Test	3′
			Completion Test	Untimed
(level A)			Silent Reading (B)	15′

Comments: The above tests represent important approaches to the assessment of speed of reading and comprehension. The standardisation and normative data are relatively unsophisticated but allow cautious comparison of children's current attainments on these tests with those on whom the data was collected. The 'One Minute Test' might appeal to a teacher's sense of economy, but has some inherent weaknesses affecting its reliability. The second and third tests employ what is currently called 'cloze' test procedure, in which the child must fill in missing words in a section of writing.

Ballard's books are now out of print, but are usually available in any library of books for teachers: (1943) *Mental Tests*, London: University of London Press, 13th reprinting; (1941) *The New Examiner*, London, 9th reprinting; *Group Tests of Intelligence*, London: University of London Press.

TRN	Name of test	Author	Country	Publisher	Publisher
10	*Burt Reading Tests 1-5*	C. Burt	B	Staples Press	1921

Type	No. of forms	C.A. range	Skills tested	Time
Individual, oral	1	5 : 0 to 14 : 0	T(1). Graded Vocabulary Test (Accuracy) (110 items)	Untimed
Individual or group, oral	1	5 : 0+	T(2). Knowledge of Letters and Figures (52 and 46 items)	Untimed
Individual, oral	1	6 : 0 to 14 : 0	T(3). Two and three letter monosyllables (200 items)	Timed and Untimed
Individual, silent	1	5 : 0 to 14 : 0	T(4). Graded Directions Test (Comprehension) (17 items)	Untimed
Individual	1	7 : 0 to 14 : 0	T(5). Continuous Prose Test (Speed, Accuracy and Comprehension)	Timed
(level A)				

Comments: These were some of the earliest reading tests devised in Britain. The standardisation and norms are understandably not comparable in sophistication with many tests available today. Yet because Burt gives data concerning the performances of children on these tests in the 1920s, the tests can help the teacher of reading appreciate what was achieved in schools at that time. The insight into the nature of the reading process shown by Burt and the importance of particular aspects of it in the teaching of reading to children are worthy of any teacher's attention. The tests are available in *Mental and Scholastic Tests* published by Staples Press. Almost any library of books for teachers will contain a copy.

TRN	Name of test		Author	Country	Publisher		Year
11	*Burt (rearranged) Word Reading Test*		C. Burt, revised by P. E. Vernon	B	Hodder and Stoughton Educational		1938 to 1954

Type	No. of forms	C.A. range	Skills tested		Time
Individual, oral	1	5 : 0 to 14 : 0	Word recognition		Untimed (10′)

(level A)

Comments: In 1938 Vernon restandardised Burt's original word recognition test for use with Scottish children. It was found necessary to rearrange the order of some of the words. The 110-word 'rearranged' test was yet again restandardised in 1954 on 6000 Edinburgh children aged from five to twelve years, and revised norms were published in 1967. The test is of doubtful value at its extremes as the initial and final ten words were arbitrarily selected to represent the ages, i.e. reading ages of four to five years and over fourteen years. The test's greatest weakness is the use of a relatively small number of items to represent a considerable change in reading attainments, one year of reading age being covered by only ten words. The ease with which raw scores can be converted to Reading Ages is a practice which appeals to teachers.

Provided they are aware of the increase of variability of reading test scores from age group to age group, the inappropriate normative comparison of children can be avoided. The test manual produced by Vernon gives details of the test's revision and discusses the differences in reading attainments in English and Scottish schools.

In 1972, Eric Shearer, an educational psychologist in Cheshire, started work on updating the word order of the test. He has also produced new norms based on a representative sample of 6000 children aged from just below five up to eleven years. These norms are currently available and according to Shearer should accurately represent contemporary national standards.

TRN	Name of test	Author	Country	Publisher	Year
14	*Comprehension Test for College of Education Students*	E. L. Black	B	NFER	1962

Type	No. of forms	C.A. range	Skills tested	Time
Attainment mainly, but with diagnostic possibilities	1	18 : 0+	Reading comprehension	60'

(level P)

Comments: The two main purposes of this test are to help in selecting students for entry to Colleges of Education and, secondly, to identify areas of weakness in which help might be provided to improve a student's skills. In the test, seven passages of reading are each followed by between seven and eleven questions, totalling sixty items in all. Multiple-choice type questions predominate.

The test was standardised in 1953 on a sample of 697 men and 911 women students in their first term at certain Colleges of Education. The internal consistency reliability of the test is high, $r = 0.939$. Satisfactory evidence of predictive validity is presented.

Recent research has suggested that the scores of College of Education students have declined significantly since 1953. This is a matter of some importance which requires further study.

TRN 17	Name of test *Domain Phonic Tests*	Author J. McLeod and J. Atkinson	Country B	Publisher Oliver and Boyd	Year 1972

Type	No. of forms	C.A. range	Skills tested	Time
Group and individual, diagnostic (level A)	1	5 : 0 to 11 : 0	P1. Simple consonants and single vowels P2. Single consonant followed by vowel blend P3. Consonant blends and single vowels P4. Vowel blends and consonant blends P5. Phonemic discrimination test	Untimed (about 10′ per test)

Comments: The aim of these tests is to enable the teacher to identify any difficulty a child might have with single-letter sounds, short and long vowels and with consonant and vowel blends. These tests are constructed by combining single vowels and consonants and the most frequently used vowel blends and consonant blends, such that each phonic unit is represented in several different words. Related to the tests is a series of exercises intended to remedy phonic weaknesses identified by the tests.

The tests appear to be based on a logical analysis of elementary phonics of importance in early reading. No evidence of reliabilities, validities or standardisation is given. In these respects the tests are similar to Jackson's *Phonic Skills* Tests. A claim based on experience rather than formal experiment is made for the effectiveness of the remedial exercises.

TRN 22	Name of test *Edinburgh Reading Tests*, Stage 1	Author Godfrey Thomson Unit for Academic Assessment	Country B	Publisher Hodder and Stoughton Educational	Year In preparation (1975)

Type	No. of forms	C.A. range	Skills tested	Time
Group and individual, attainment and diagnostic (level A)	2 (A & B)	7 : 0 to 9 : 0	Reading attainments in a number of areas deemed important at this stage of reading acquisition. Currently under discussion	Timed

Comments: I am informed that the nucleus of a team has been formed to start work on Stage 1 of this series, but that the test is unlikely to be published before Easter 1976.

TRN	Name of test	Author	Country	Publisher	Year
23	*Edinburgh Reading Tests, Stage 2*	Godfrey Thomson Unit, University of Edinburgh	B	Hodder and Stoughton Educational	1972

Type	No. of forms	C.A. range	Skills tested	Time
Group and individual,	1	8 : 6 to 10 : 6	Practice Test (untimed)	(30')
attainment and diagnostic	1		Part 1	
			A. Vocabulary	12'
			B. Comprehension of sequences	12'
			C. Retention of significant detail	12'
	1		Part 2	
			D. Use of context	12'
			E. Reading rate	2'
			F. Comprehension of essential ideas	16'
(level A)			Total Score	

Comments: This was the first of the proposed four tests in the series to become available. Its purpose is to provide the teacher with information concerning children's reading attainments that will help her in adapting methods and materials to facilitate children's acquisition of reading skills. The test constructors consider reading to be a unified ability which most children tend to be good or bad at as a whole. Thus the handbook stresses great caution in the interpretation of the profiles obtained: 'most children need help right across the board, and not in one ability more than in any other' (Manual, p. 29). The test manual advocates that, for children with low scores on any sub-test (except E), the teacher can go through the test individually with the child in an attempt to discover what it was that the child found difficult: 'if he gets an answer wrong, ask him why he thinks his answer is right' (*Ibid*, p. 29). The danger of 'teaching the test' would appear very near in such a situation. If the test were a mastery or criterion-referenced test, this might not matter. In a normative test, such an approach, if used extensively, could make future interpretation of the scores difficult.

As would be expected of the Godfrey Thomson Unit, the standardisation on both English and Scottish children is clearly reported. The total score and the sub-tests all (excepting E) have high internal consistency reliabilities. Sex differences and nationality differences in scores are discussed and reported. The manual allows conversion of raw scores into standard scores for *Total* scores only, for each month of age between 8 : 6 and 10 : 6. For the sub-tests, scores are awarded *only* to allow comparison between the different aspects of a given child's performance. Hence no age allowance is included on sub-test conversion tables. This distinction must be borne in mind by test users, or else unjustified inter-individual comparisons on sub-test scores might be made between children of different age groups. The manual is helpful on the content of the sub-scales and the interpretation that is suggested when certain items are failed.

The administration of the test requires considerable care and accurate timing.

Potentially, the test looks a valuable one likely to be used extensively in the UK, in particular by teachers concerned with identifying and helping children with reading difficulties.

F

TRN	Name of test	Author	Country	Publisher	Year
24	*Edinburgh Reading Tests, Stage 3*	Moray House College of Education	B	Hodder and Stoughton Educational	1972

Type	No. of forms	C.A. range	Skills tested	Time
Group and individual, attainment and diagnostic	I	10 : 0 to 12 : 6	Practice Test (untimed)	(35′)
	I		Part 1.	
			A. Reading for facts	10′
			B. Comprehension of sequences	10′
			C. Retention of main ideas	10′
	I		Part 2.	
			D. Comprehension of points of view	15′
(level A)			E. Vocabulary	10′

Comments: Fergus McBride, Lecturer in Education at Moray House, and P. C. McNaught have been concerned with the construction of this test. It is intended to give an overall measure of a child's general reading competence and also a profile for each child in the five areas indicated above. The test has been standardised on random samples of 2865 children in Scotland and 2793 in England and Wales, excluding children in special schools containing pupils of very low reading ability. The manual currently available gives data on total score and sub-test reliabilities (internal consistency). Total score reliability was 0·97 and sub-test reliabilities ranged from 0·81 to 0·95. No information on validities is available other than that the content validity rests on the judgment of reading experts. It is anticipated that other validation data will become available later.

Children's raw scores can be converted to reading quotients with a mean of 100 and a standard deviation of 15. Reading ages can also be obtained for Scottish and English and Welsh children. The manual discusses profile interpretation in very general terms, but gives no suggestions to help the teacher interpret particular patterns. Guidance is given on the interpretation of individual sub-test results. The high intercorrelations of the sub-tests (0·709 to 0·838) suggest that a common core of reading abilities is sampled by all sub-tests. This makes profile interpretation extremely difficult.

There are plans to extend this series of tests by a further stage, 4, intended to cover the age range twelve to sixteen years.

TRN 27	Name of test GAP Reading Comprehension Test	Author J. McLeod and D. Unwin	Country B	Publisher Heinemann Educational	Year 1970

Type Constructed response, attainment	No. of forms 2 (B & R)	C.A. range 8 : 0 to 12 : 0	Skills tested Reading comprehension	Time 15′

(level A)

Comments: The GAP test presents a series of seven short passages of writing with certain words omitted. The child has to *construct* his own response. The correctness of the response is judged against the criterion of the response of 'good readers'. No penalty is exacted for spelling a semantically correct response incorrectly.

The test was originally standardised in Australia on a sample of 2029 children aged from 7 : 0 to 12 : 0. The test has been used on over 1000 children attending schools in Great Britain with results comparable to those obtained in Australia. The norms presented are based on the British sample and provide reading ages ranging from 7 : 5 to 12 : 6. Australian evidence of test-retest reliability and concurrent validity is presented. A concurrent validity coefficient of 0.73 showing the correlation between the GAP test score and *Schonell Reading Test B* for the British sample is reported. The details of the standardisation and of the test's reliabilities and validities are meagre.

Some teachers might have reservations about penalising children who produce a plausible response rather than the one(s) prescribed by the authors on the basis of 'good readers'' responses. Despite this comment, the simplicity of the test will appeal to many teachers requiring an assessment of a child's reading comprehension of continuous prose.

TRN	Name of test	Author	Country	Publisher	Year
28	*GAPADOL Reading Comprehension Test*	J. McLeod and J. Anderson	B/A	Heinemann Educational	1973

Type	No. of forms	C.A. range	Skills tested	Time
Constructed response, attainment	2 (G & Y)	7 : 3 to 16 : 11	Reading comprehension	30′

(level A)

Comments: The GAPADOL test consists of six passages of writing with certain words omitted. The child has to construct responses that fit the gaps, of which there are 81 and 83 in Forms G and Y respectively. The adequacy of a child's response is judged against the criterion of the response of 'good readers'. Incorrect spellings are not penalised.

The manual is extremely brief. It refers readers wanting information concerning the construction and standardisation of the test to other sources. The evidence of reliabilities presented is presumably based on Australian children. Internal consistency reliabilities and the standard errors of measurement are given for each year of chronological age, with the exception of the age range 8 : 3 to 9 : 3 which appears to have been (inadvertently?) omitted. The coefficients presented range from 0·84 to 0·92. No evidence of validities is presented in the manual.

Raw scores can be converted directly to reading ages. For each month of chronological age from 7 : 3 to 16 : 11 raw scores indicating the norm for the age group and also of the 90th and 10th percentile ranks are presented. The latter is interpreted as showing 'retardation' in reading.

As with the *GAP Reading Comprehension Test*, some teachers would have reservations about penalising a child who produced a response that was semantically correct but not precisely that response produced by 'good readers'. Despite this reservation, the simplicity of the test is likely to appeal to many teachers. Presumably English norms will be developed in time.

TRN	Name of test	Author	Country	Publisher	Year
37	*Graded Word Reading Test*	P. E. Vernon	B	Hodder and Stoughton Educational	1938

Type	No. of forms	C.A. range	Skills tested	Time
Individual, oral, attainment (level A)	1	6 : 0 to 18 : 0	Word reading	Untimed (10′)

Comments: In Glasgow, Vernon devised a word reading test of 130 words producing reading ages ranging from five years (raw score of 0) to twenty-one years (raw score of 130). Both the first fourteen and the last thirty words of the test are particularly suspect. Bearing in mind the year when it was produced, the manual gives considerable details of the standardisation procedure and of the test's reliabilities and validities. Vernon points out how weaknesses in the standardisation procedure at various age levels and in the selection of words causes difficulty in interpreting the test results. Not the least of these arises from the use of 'reading ages'. It is likely that his openness in this respect has resulted in the test's relatively infrequent use by teachers. Reading ages have an appealing simplicity that can be misleading.

TRN	Name of test		Author		Country	Publisher		Year
39	*Group Reading Assessment*		F. A. Spooncer		B	Hodder and Stoughton Educational		1964

Type	No. of forms	C.A. range	Skills tested	Time
Group, attainment	I	7 : 8 to 9 : 0	Word recognition	30′
			Sentence reading	
(level A)				

Comments: The test consists of three parts. In the first sixteen items, the teacher says a word contained in a suggested sentence and the child has to draw a line under one of five words in the printed test booklet. The twenty-five items in part 2 are sentence completion from multiple-choice. In part 3 the children are presented with rows of words in which at least two words, although spelt differently, sound the same. The task is for the child to underline the words which have the same sound as the first word in the row, e.g. 'too: two, low, ton, to, chew'. There are sixteen of these items. This test is intended to assess the reading level of children at the end of their first year in the Junior school. Its content was determined after discussions with teachers as to which aspects of reading they considered important. Thus both mechanical aspects of reading and reading comprehension were sampled. The validity data presented suggests that the test fulfils its primary aim of testing mechanical reading rather than comprehension. The reliability (internal consistency) of the test is high, 0·969 for the whole test. Test-retest reliability after an eight-month interval was 0·91. It is suggested by Spooncer that the test should not be used during the Autumn term of the first year in the Junior school as some children find difficulties in following the instructions at that stage.

TRN	Name of test		Author	Country	Publisher		Year
40	*Group Reading Test*		D. Young	B	Hodder and Stoughton Educational		1968

Type	No. of forms	C.A. range	Skills tested		Time
Multiple-choice, group, attainment	2 (A & B)	6 : 6 to 12 : 11	1. Word-picture matching		20′
			2. Reading comprehension		(including practice)
(level A)					

Comments: Each form of Young's test comprises forty-five items. In fifteen of these items *one* of between three and five words must be selected to match a picture. In the next thirty items the child is looking for synonyms in multiple-choice sentence-completion format. Although this forty-five-item test is standardised on over 7400 children aged from 6 : 6 to 12 : 11, over the age of ten years, 50 per cent of the children were *above* the test's ceiling. This makes for difficulties in producing acceptable standard scores. Young presents evidence of reliability using the standard error of the reading coefficients. These appear acceptable, as is the evidence for different types of validity reported. A major weakness of this test lies, perhaps, in trying to cover reading attainment over such a large age range with such a relatively small number of items. This inevitably leads to difficulties in constructing norms and also in interpreting them. Young's consideration of the equivalence of test scores on some of the most commonly used instruments* is of value to the teacher attempting to relate scores on Young's tests to ones with which she may be more familiar.

* *Neale Analysis of Reading Ability;* NFER *Reading Test BD* (formerly *Sentence Reading Test 1*); *Southgate Group Reading Test 1.*

TRN	Name of test	Author	Country	Publisher	Year
42	*Holborn Reading Scale*	A. F. Watts	B	G. G. Harrap and Co. Ltd	1948

Type	No. of forms	C.A. range	Skills tested	Time
Individual, oral (word recognition), silent (comprehension)	1	5 : 6 to 11 : 0	Word recognition Comprehension	Untimed (20'-30')

(level A)

Comments: The scale comprises thirty-three sentences in increasing order of difficulty in terms of word recognition and comprehension. Each sentence represents a reading age three months higher than the preceding sentence. A child's mechanical reading ability can be rapidly assessed, but there are no norms for comprehension; hence the comparison between a child's mechanical reading and comprehension cannot be made as meaningfully as is suggested in the manual. There is no mention of reliability or validity in the manual. The norms are dated. This test has achieved popularity perhaps because of its ease of administration and the apparently simple interpretation of scores. It also offers the possibility of comparing a pupil's oral reading and silent reading comprehension of the same sentence by answering related questions.

TRN	Name of test	Author	Country	Publisher	Year
47	*Kelvin Measurement of Reading Ability*	C. M. Fleming	B	R. Gibson and Son Ltd	1933

Type	No. of forms	C.A. range	Skills tested	Time
Individual or group, attainment	1	8 : 0 to 12 : 0	Reading comprehension	20'

(level A)

Comments: This test consists of five separate paragraphs. For each, the child is given four minutes to read and answer four questions in the test booklet. Raw scores can be converted to percentiles, standard scores and reading ages. No evidence on reliabilities or validities is presented.

TRN	Name of test		Author	Country	Publisher		Year
47a	*Key Words Attainment and Diagnostic Test*		J. McNally	B	Schoolmaster Publishing Co. Ltd		1968

Type	No. of forms	C.A. range	Skills tested	Time
Content criterion-referenced, group and individual	1	5 : 00+	A. Word recognition (group)	Untimed
			Bi. Word recognition (individual)	1′
			ii. Timed reading of first ten lines of list	timed
			C. Word recognition:	
			comparison of speed of reading and word attack on	
			phonically regular and irregular words respectively.	
(level A)				

Comments: The above test is based on the 200 words most frequently in common use, as identified by McNally and Murray (1962).* Early incorporation of these words into a reader's sight vocabulary is considered vital by these authors. McNally describes three major ways in which the specially devised test card can be used. Variations in the administration of tests A, B and C of diagnostic importance are described. Because the test is content criterion-referenced, none of the norms or indices of reliability and validity typically provided with normative tests, are given. It is suggested that in tests B and C, teachers can establish their own norms for subsequent use. Because the test is a mastery test, the teacher is perfectly justified in teaching to her pupils such of the words in the test as she considers appropriate to her pupils' needs. The success of the teaching and of the pupils' learning will be reflected in changes in pupils' raw scores on the tests.

*McNally, J. and Murray, W. (1962) *Key Words to Literacy*. Curriculum Studies No. 3., London: Schoolmaster Publishing Co. Ltd.

TRN	Name of test	Author	Country	Publisher	Year
48	*Kingston Test of Silent Reading*	M. E. Hebron	B	G. G. Harrap and Co. Ltd	1954

Type	No. of forms	C.A. range	Skills tested	Time
Group, attainment	1	7 : 0 to 10 : 11	Silent reading comprehension	20'

(level A)

Comments: This test is in the form of a 600-word continuous story with fifty-two words omitted. The child's task is to read the story and write down as many of the missing words as he can in the time allowed. Thus the test is designed in terms of 'cloze' procedure (see page 21).

The test was standardised on some 2000 second-year Junior school pupils plus 'smaller representative groups' at other age levels. The test is more suitable for use with children aged 8 : 6 and older than with younger ones. With older children the internal consistency coefficient of reliability is 0·96. Parallel form reliability would probably be lower. A conversion table enables raw scores to be converted to deviation scores with a mean of 100 and a standard deviation of 15. Correlations of reading test scores with other mental test scores are given, but nothing is said about the meaning of these intercorrelations.

TRN	Name of test	Author	Country	Publisher	Year
49	*Manchester Reading Comprehension Test (Senior) 1*	S. Wiseman and J. Wrigley	B	University of London Press	1959

Type	No. of forms	C.A. range	Skills tested	Time
Group, attainment	1	13 : 6 to 15 : 2	Reading comprehension	45'

(level A)

Comments: This test is made up of eight passages of writing of widely varying styles. The number of questions asked per passage ranges from four to sixteen. The test was standardised on a complete age group of pupils in the Greater Manchester area. The test has very high internal consistency and test-retest reliabilities. It is validated against the Watts-Vernon test used in the Department of Education and Science's surveys of reading ability reported in DES Pamphlets 18 and 32. Raw scores can be converted to standard scores for each month of age. There are separate norms for boys and girls.

This is an excellent test of reading comprehension. It is difficult to understand why the test was not used more extensively in the schools in which it was standardised and, in consequence, is no longer generally available.

TRN	Name of test	Author	Country	Publisher	Year
57	*NFER Prawf Darllen Brawddegan 1* (Welsh Sentence Reading Test)	G. J. Evans	B	NFER	1959

Type	No. of forms	C.A. range	Skills tested	Time
Group or individual, multiple-choice sentence-completion, attainment	1	8 : 0 to 10 : 11	Reading comprehension	20'

(level A)

Comments: This test is in Welsh. It consists of thirty-five graded sentences presented as multiple-choice sentence-completion items. The test was standardised in 1959 on a sample of about 2500 Welsh-speaking school children. It is an acceptably reliable instrument, its internal consistency reliability being 0·93 and the standard error of measurement being 4·0.

TRN	Name of test	Author	Country	Publisher	Year
58	*NFER Reading Test A*	NFER Guidance and Assessment Service	B	NFER	1972

Type	No. of forms	C.A. range	Skills tested	Time
Group or individual, multiple-choice sentence-completion, attainment	1	7 : 0 to 8 : 10	Reading comprehension	Untimed (20'-30')

(level A)

Comments: This test is comprised of thirty-eight simple sentence-completion type items printed in an eight-page booklet. The child has to select the correct word or phrase from four alternatives. The test is preceded by four practice items.

At present provisional norms only are available for urban children in the Midlands, South, North East and North West of England. Further normative data are being collected and national norms for the test will then be produced. The provisional test handbook is extremely brief, partly because the test is still being developed. Currently, no data on reliability or validity are available, but it can be expected that the test will measure up to the NFER's rigorous standards.

TRN	Name of test	Author	Country	Publisher	Year
59	*NFER Reading Test AD*	A. F. Watts	B	NFER	1954

Type	No. of forms	C.A. range	Skills tested	Time
Group or individual, multiple-choice sentence-completion, attainment	1	7 : 6 to 11 : 1	Reading comprehension	15′ plus 5′ practice

(level A)

Comments: The test consists of thirty-five multiple-choice sentence-completion type items printed in a four-page booklet. The test proper is preceded by four practice items. Raw scores are converted to standard scores for each month of chronological age. Thus the relative normative performances of children of differing ages can be compared. For example, a raw score of twenty-four items correct is equivalent to a standard score of 100 for a child aged 9 : 6. For an eleven-year-old child, a raw score of twenty-four items converts to a standard score of eighty-nine. Girls appear to find the test easier than boys, but there are not separate norms for boys and girls. A correction for guessing is included in the marking instructions. The manual indicates that the test is extremely reliable, although less so at the extremes of the range. No evidence of validities is presented, although the face validity of such a test of reading comprehension will convince the majority of teachers. Although the current test manual is dated 1970, the data on which the norms were constructed was obtained in 1954. A Welsh version of the above test is available (see *NFER Prawf Darllen Brawddegan*).

TRN	Name of test	Author	Country	Publisher	Year
60	*NFER Reading Test BD*	NFER Guidance and Assessment Service	B	NFER	1969

Type	No. of forms	C.A. range	Skills tested	Time
Multiple-choice, sentence-completion, attainment (level A)	1	7 : 0 to 10 : 4	Reading comprehension	20′ plus 5′-10′ practice

Comments: This is a forty-four-item test of reading comprehension. Its multiple-choice format leaves a gap in the middle of a sentence, the child having to identify the correct response from a five-option choice given at the end. The test was standardised in 1969 on a sample of about 19000 children aged from 7 : 0 to 10 : 4.   Provisional norms are also available for ages 10 : 0 to 11 : 11. There is some discrepancy between the description of the standardisation sample given in the manual and that given in the NFER Catalogue. The test does not include any correction for guessing as investigations suggested that this was unnecessary. The test-retest and internal consistency reliabilities are high. It is pointed out that comparison of the normative results with tests constructed much earlier (e.g. the Watts, standardised in 1954) could be misleading. Sex differences in test scores were found. Separate conversion tables are given for age ranges 7 : 0 to 7 : 9, 7 : 10 to 8 : 8, 8 : 0 to 8 : 9, 8 : 10 to 9 : 7 and 9 : 8 to 10 : 4. Provisional norms only are available for the age range 10 : 0 to 10 : 9. The same norms are used for both boys and girls. Validity was studied by comparing test scores for various methods of marking with teachers' estimates of reading ability as part of the investigation into the effects of guessing.

TRN	Name of test	Author	Country	Publisher	Year
61	*NFER Reading Comprehension Test DE*	E. L. Barnard	B	NFER	1967

Type	No. of forms	C.A. range	Skills tested	Time
Group, diagnostic and attainment	1	10 : 0 to 12 : 6	1. Reading comprehension (Global Understanding)	Untimed (50')
			2. Extraction of facts from a relatively complex sentence or series of sentences (Detail)	
			3. Ability to make inferences from the facts presented (Inference)	
(level A)			4. Understanding of the use of individual words or phrases	

Comments: The test is made up of eight varied passages of writing of increasing complexity, each on a separate page. Between four and eight questions are asked after each passage, some of them being open-ended. The number of questions totals fifty in all. The children's total scores can be converted to percentiles. Separate provisional norms are provided for boys and girls in the age range of 10 : 0 to 10 : 11. For the age range 11 : 0 to 11 : 11 only joint norms are available. It is suggested that the children's individual scripts can usefully be studied to see which of the four skills are dealt with most adequately. 9/50 questions relate to 'Global Understanding', 22/50 to 'Detail', 11/50 to 'Inference' and 8/50 to the 'Use of individual words or phrases'. The provisional manual issued in 1971 contains no evidence of reliability or validity. The test was standardised on a relatively small number of children and the tentative norms should be used with caution. The diagnostic use of the information available from the four highly related skills that are tested appears rather nebulous, though one can discern possibilities for the experienced clinician. It is surprising that a test should be issued by the NFER with so poor a manual. One must assume that the final version will avoid the weaknesses in the provisional manual and that as reputable an organisation as the NFER has sound evidence available for the reliability, validity and diagnostic potential of this interesting test.

TRN	Name of test	Author	Country	Publisher	Year
62	*NFER Reading Test EH*	S. M. Bate	B	NFER	1961
					1961
					1965

Type	No. of forms	C.A. range	Skills tested	Time
Test 1—Sentence-completion, multiple-choice	1	11 : 6 to 15 : 6	Test 1: Vocabulary—reading comprehension	Untimed (20′)
Test 2—Paragraph reading plus questions	1		Test 2: Comprehension	Untimed (30′)
Test 3—Continuous prose	1		Test 3: Speed of reading	4½′-7′

(level A)

Comments: Test 1 consists of sixty multiple-choice sentence-completion items; Test 2 contains seven paragraphs of writing each followed by five questions, mainly multiple-choice; Test 3 is made up of two extracts, one from *Aku-Aku* by Heyerdahl and the other from *The Story of San Michele* by Munthe. In Test 3 a series of multiple-choices are inserted into the extracts, the last point the child has underlined being used as the basis on which his speed of reading is assessed. These tests were provisionally standardised in 1966 on a group of children aged 11 : 0 to 15 : 6.

The manual for this test is, as yet, still in its provisional form. Raw scores can be converted to standard scores for each test and separate conversion tables are given for Year 1, Year 2 and Years 3 and 4 combined. No evidence of reliabilities or validities is presented, but presumably will appear when the final form of the manual is available. The process appears to be unduly protracted in this particular instance.

TRN	Name of test	Author	Country	Publisher	Year
63	*NFER Tests of English Proficiency for Immigrant Children*	National Foundation for Educational Research	B	NFER	1973

Type	No. of forms	C.A. range	Skills tested	Levels of Linguistic Analysis					Time
Group or individual, diagnostic, content criterion-referenced		7 : 0 to 11 : 0		1	2	3	4	5	Some timed, some not
	1		Listening comprehension skills		*(33)	*(28)	*(30)		
	1		Speaking skills (individual)		*(25)	*(15)	*(11)		
	1		Reading skills		*(33)	*(28)	*(28)		
	1		Writing skills		*(25)	*(20)	*(11)		
(level A)			(*Levels at which tests are available. No. of items in brackets)						

Comments: The above tests, with colour-coded booklets for ease of identification, are designed for use with immigrants whose native tongue or dialect differs from the English used in schools. Such children may require special placement and instruction. The tests have been constructed on a linguistic analysis of language as sets of five hier-archically-related skills in the four areas shown above, level 1 being the most elementary in each case. There are only three main tests in each area, tapping those parts of the language model shown by asterisks above. These tests are, rather misleadingly, labelled 'Listening 1, 2 and 3', etc. The first tests in all areas use a common core of twelve nouns and eight verbs. Listening 2 and Reading 2 share ten common items. Taped instructions are used in Listening 2 and 3. The child's individual responses to Speaking 1, 2 and 3 are tape-recorded. The Speaking Tests are parallel to the Writing Tests and are scored similarly.

The use of a content criterion-referenced testing model is interesting, but as there is no evidence from a native-speaking group, one has some doubts as to the validity of the criteria of mastery given for each test. Additionally, the reasons for not giving some of the reliabilities of the tests are suspect. The intercorrelations of the tests are not given. The tests sample a wide range of elementary patterns and may conceivably have value with members of the host population who have language difficulties. However, the need to key such tests to educational pro-grammes that are shown to be effective is of paramount importance. These tests are likely to achieve considerable popularity with teachers of immigrant pupils.

TRN	Name of test	Author		Country	Publisher	Year
64	*Neale Analysis of Reading Ability*	M. D. Neale		B	Macmillan and Co. Ltd	1957-8

Type	No. of forms	C.A. range	Skills tested	Time
Individual, oral, diagnostic	3 (A, B & C)	6 : 0 to 12 : 0	Main test:	20'
			Reading accuracy	
			Reading speed	
			Reading comprehension	
			Subsidiary tests:	
			Names and sounds of letters	
			Auditory discrimination	
(level P)			Syllable blending and recognition	

Comments: Each form of the test contains six short stories of increasing length and complexity. Questions are asked after each story. There is an individual record sheet of four pages for each form of the test. An analysis of the child's errors can be made as he is reading.

The manual gives evidence of satisfactory reliability of the main test accuracy scores.

Although validation of the comprehension scale is not completely satisfactory, the test has been found of value by clinicians and remedial teachers in particular.

TRN	Name of Test	Author	Country	Publisher	Year
66	*Phonic Skills (P.S.) Tests*	S. Jackson	B	Robert Gibson and Sons Ltd, Glasgow	1971

Type	No. of forms	C.A. range	Skills tested	Time
Individual and group, diagnostic, criterion-referenced	1	5 : 0 to 10 : 0	1. Sounds, names, initial sounds, final sounds (lower-case letters, group test)	Untimed
			2. Sounds, names (upper-case letters, group test)	
			3. Individual letters (lower case, individual test)	
			4. Individual letters (upper case, individual test)	
			5. Two- and three-letter words	
			6. Final consonant blends	
			7. Initial consonant blends	
			8. Vowel digraphs	
			9. Consonant digraphs	
			10. Word endings	
(level A)			11. Multi-syllabic words	

Comments: Jackson has devised a series of eleven reading tests of the phonic skills he considers important in reading. These tests enable the teacher to identify the skills with which a child has difficulties. The results of whichever tests are administered are recorded on a Phonic Skills Record Card. Guidance is given in the interpretation of test results and in developing individual remedial programmes for each child. These suggestions are based on Jackson's considerable experience and knowledge. This series of tests is apparently based on a logical analysis of the component phonic skills involved in reading. It has much in common with the Stott *Programmed Reading Kit* (1971). Jackson's series of tests can be looked upon as a checklist of important skills or as a series of mastery tests. There is no evidence given at all concerning standardisation (one suspects that none was carried out), reliabilities and validities. No evidence is presented for the efficacy of the remedial treatment he suggests. It is a pity that such information is not provided. The major reason for including this series of tests is that they represent a recent analysis of the possible phonic skills involved in reading. The tests are likely to be of value to the teacher who is concerned with diagnosing and rectifying the weaknesses in phonic skills of her children. Jackson's suggestions for remedial work, in *Get Reading Right: a handbook for remedial teachers*, have been favourably received by many teachers.

TRN	Name of test	Author	Country	Publisher	Year
72	*Reading Comprehension Test for Personnel Selection*	L. R. C. Haward	B	Hodder and Stoughton Educational	1965

Type	No. of forms	C.A. range	Skills tested		Time
Group or individual, attainment (level A)	1	15 : 0+	Extraction of information from a technical text		15'

Comments: This twenty-five-item test is intended to help in the selection of students over fifteen years of age wishing to take further courses of training that depend upon an extensive use of textbooks. To this end it has been used in the selection of 'nurses, technical apprentices and foreign immigrants as well as in the field of further education'. The test comprises a passage from a textbook followed by twenty-five questions which test students' ability to obtain information from a technical text.

The standardisation of the test is based on a very small sample. In calculating the item characteristics, only item facility appears to have been considered; no attention was apparently paid to item discrimination. The test is reported as having high split-half and test-retest reliabilities. The data for the test's predictive validities are not impressive although concurrent validity appears rather higher. The data on which suggested cut-off points for predictions of future course success, partial failure and failure are based appear rather slender.

TRN	Name of test	Author	Country	Publisher	Year
75	*Salford Sentence Reading Tests*	G. Bookbinder	B	Under negotiation	In preparation (1975)

Type	No. of forms	C.A. range	Skills tested		Time
Individual, oral, attainment (level A)	3 (A, B & C)	6 : 0 to 10 : 0	Sentence reading		Untimed (5')

Comments: This test consists of thirteen progressively more complex sentences. The child's task is to read these aloud to the tester until six errors have been made. The test is easily and quickly administered.

Standardisation was carried out on a sample of 250 children whose reading attainments were equivalent to national standards. Inter-form reliability is high. No other evidence of reliabilities or validities is given, but is being obtained (personal communication). *All* children with reading ages of less than six years are classed only as 'below six years'.

This test is similar to the *Holborn Sentence Reading Test* but has the advantages of parallel forms.

TRN	Name of test	Author	Country	Publisher	Year
76	*Schonell Reading Tests*	F. J. Schonell and F. E. Schonell	B	Oliver and Boyd	1942 to 1955

Type	No. of forms	C.A. range	Skills tested	Time
Individual, oral	1	5 : 0 to 15 : 0	R1. Graded Word Reading	5'-15'
Individual	1	6 : 0 to 9 : 0	R2. Simple Prose Reading Test ('My Dog')	3'-8'
Group	1	7 : 0 to 11 : 0	R3. Silent Reading Test A	15'
Group	1	9 : 0 to 13 : 0	R4. Silent Reading Test B	20'
Individual	1		R5. Analysis and synthesis of words containing common phonic units	5'-15'
Individual	1		R6. Directional attack on words	5'-10'
Individual	1		R7. Visual Word Discrimination Test	10'-15'

(level A)

Comments: These tests form a battery for the assessment of reading attainment (R1 to R4) and for the diagnosis of aspects of failure in some of the mechanics of reading (R5 to R7). The last three tests have no norms. Information on the standardisation, reliability and validity of the tests is noticeable by its absence. The norms of tests R1 to R4 are dated but for R1 have recently been revised (1972). The diagnostic tests do not include a number of aspects of reading now considered important, e.g. auditory discrimination between words, matching written and heard forms of words.

The battery was designed for use by teachers and specialists in the teaching of reading. It proved a useful tool in its day. Teachers who have built up the necessary experience for the interpretation of the results from tests R5 to R7 will doubtless continue to use them.

Test R1, the *Schonell Graded Word Reading Test*, is one of the most widely used in the UK. The publishers issued new norms in 1972 based on a small sample of specially selected children attending schools in Salford. Recently Eric Shearer, an educational psychologist working in Cheshire, has administered the test to a nationally representative sample of 6000 children aged from below five up to eleven years attending Cheshire schools. He has been able to revise the order of difficulty of the words and to restandardise the norms for the test. Shearer claims that the new norms are remarkably similar to those produced by Schonell over thirty years ago, but are very different from those given in the 1972 norms issued by the publishers.

TRN	Name of test	Author	Country	Publisher	Year
78	*Southgate Group Reading Tests 1 and 2*	V. Southgate	B	Hodder and Stoughton Educational	Test 1, 1959 Test 2, 1962

Type	No. of forms	C.A. range	Skills tested	Time
1. Group, oral administration, attainment	3 (A, B & C)	6 : 0 to 7 : 6	1. Word selection	Untimed
2. Group, attainment	2 (A & B)	7 : 0 to 8 : 11	2. Sentence-completion (comprehension)	15'-20'

(level A)

Comments: Test 1 is a thirty-item test specially devised for use with children in the early stages of reading acquisition. It was standardised on a group consisting of every child aged from 5 : 8 to 8 : 1 in Local Educational Authority schools in Worcester in 1957. The test is contained in an illustrated booklet. Sixteen of the thirty items involve selecting a word to match a picture named by the tester. In the other items the children have to underline, from sets of five, one word dictated by the tester. Testing in groups of no more than fifteen to twenty children is advised. It is also claimed that the test can be used with older children having difficulty with reading. The results are expressed in reading ages from 5 : 9 to 7 : 9.

Test 2 is a test of reading comprehension and can be administered to classes. Form A is printed in white and Form B in blue, hence cheating can readily be minimised. Each form consists of forty-two sentences with a choice of five words of which the child must choose one to complete the sentence. Norms are given for reading ages from 7 : 0 to 9 : 7 and in percentiles. The accompanying manuals give clear instructions and also evidence of satisfactory reliabilities and validities. These tests have been extensively used in national and local surveys.

TRN	Name of test	Author	Country	Publisher	Year
78a	SPAR (*Spelling and Reading*) Tests	D. Young	B	Hodder and Stoughton Educational	1976

Type	No. of forms	C.A. Range	Skills tested	Time
Normative, group, attainment and diagnostic	Spelling: a number of parallel forms can be constructed	7 : 0 to 15 : 11	Spelling (30 items)	Untimed
(level A)	Reading: 2 (A & B)	7 : 0 to 15 : 11	Reading: picture-word matching sentence completion	4' 9'

Comments: The SPAR tests are intended to assess the progress towards literacy in both spelling and reading of the majority of junior school pupils and of less able secondary school pupils.

From two item banks, each of 150 words, the teacher can construct ten parallel spelling tests without any overlap in content, and a far larger number with partial overlap.

The reading test follows the same format as the author's *Group Reading Test* (TRN 40). Raw scores on both the spelling and reading tests can be converted to attainment ages and quotients. The standardisation of the tests at the junior school stage is on pupils in schools known to be representative of national attainment standards on various NFER and Moray House tests. At this age band, 1864 and 3797 pupils were involved in the standardisation of the spelling and reading tests

respectively. At the secondary level the norms are based on the same 936 pupils for each test, but the norms are derived by an undescribed method of calibration from nationally standardised tests. Various indices of reliability and validity are presented for various groups of pupils, mostly for the junior groups.

It is particularly useful to have at the secondary-school level tests of spelling and reading based on the *same* group of slow-learning pupils. This allows a more adequate consideration of intra-individual differences in attainments on these two important aspects of literacy. Despite reporting sex differences in attainments in these tests, Young has decided to present combined norms as these '. . . are of greater practical value to the practising teacher than separate tables of norms . . .'.

TRN	Name of test	Author	Country	Publisher	Year
79	*Standard Reading Tests*	J. C. Daniels and Hunter Diack	B	Chatto and Windus Ltd	1958

Type	No. of forms	C.A. range	Skills tested	Time
Test 1, individual, oral,	1	5 : 0 to 9 : 0*	1. The standard test of reading skill	Untimed
attainment	1	initial stages	2. Copying abstract figures	Untimed
Tests 2-10, individual,	1	of reading	3. Copying a sentence	Untimed
diagnostic	1		4. Visual discrimination and orientation	Untimed
Test 11, group or individual	1		5. Letter recognition test	Untimed
diagnostic and attainment	1		6. Aural discrimination test	Untimed
Test 12, attainment, group	8		7. Diagnostic word-recognition tests	Untimed
	1		8. Oral word-recognition tests	Untimed
	1		9. Picture word-recognition tests	Untimed
	1		10. Silent prose-reading and comprehension test	Untimed
	1	5 : 0 to 12 : 3*	11. Graded spelling test	Untimed
	1	6 : 0 to 14 : 0*	12. Graded test of reading experience	20'

(level A)   * Reading attainment ages covered by the test norms.

Comments: The twelve tests come in a convenient book form. Only Tests 1, 11 and 12 have norms. Test 1 is made up of thirty-six sentences in question form but is only scored for accuracy of reading. The items are arranged in a statistically derived order of difficulty which also reflects increasing content difficulty from the point of view of a logical analysis of reading.

The reading age range covered is from 5 : 0 to 9 : 0. Test 11 is a spelling test giving spelling ages from 5 : 0 to 12 : 3. Test 12 is a multiple-choice sentence-completion group test giving reading ages from 6 : 0 to 14 : 0, although norms above the ten-year-old level are unreliable.

The manual contains no details of the standardisation procedure or of the test reliabilities or validities, which makes it difficult to interpret the results. The nine diagnostic tests cover a wide range of abilities underlying reading attainments. The instructions for administration of the tests are clear and the interpretation of results indicated in the handbook seem to have been of value. Despite serious limitations in the technical aspects of the handbook, many teachers have found this battery of tests a great help in individual diagnostic work. It is now in its eighth impression, which gives an indication of its popularity.

TRN	Name of test	Author	Country	Publisher	Year
81	*Swansea Test of Phonic Skills* (experimental version)	P. Williams, with the assistance of P. Congdon, M. Holder and N. Sims	B	Basil Blackwell Ltd, Oxford	1972

Type	No. of forms	C.A. range	Skills tested	Time

Group or individual, diagnostic	1	5 : 9 to 7 : 9 (standardisation sample)	1. Short vowels
			2. Long vowels
			3. Initial letter blends
			4. Final letter blends
			5. Miscellaneous:
			  (*a*) vowel combinations
			  (*b*) consonant digraphs, initial position
			  (*c*) consonant digraphs, final position
				40′

(level A)

Comments: This test was developed as one aspect of the Schools Council Research and Development Project in Compensatory Education centred at Swansea University. The test is primarily intended for children having reading ages of below 7 : 6. The phonic skills tested are seen as of particular interest to those teaching reading to children from low socio-economic backgrounds. The authors also recommend its use with children in remedial reading groups, in slow-learning classes and with top infant and young junior school children whose reading is causing concern. The test consists of sixty-five items. Each item is a *nonsense* word placed with four alternatives. The child has to ring the printed nonsense word when the tester utters it. The manual has some weaknesses. For example, the instructions for administration give no reference to the appendix listing the specified stimulus words. In view of the specific focus of the study which resulted in these tests, the rather sparse information on standardisation and reliability is understandable. Evidence of validities is presented and further studies are in hand. The information on interpretation of the results, which are in effect profiles, is kept extremely simple. The reliabilities and inter-correlations of the sub-test scores are not given. The scores are used to see whether a child has mastered a series of definable reading skill objectives. Raw scores can also be related to *Southgate Group Reading Test* scores.

It is accepted that this test is still in an experimental stage. It looks as if it has some promise.

TRN	Name of test	Author	Country	Publisher	Year
86	*Watts' Battery of Language and Reading Tests*	A. F. Watts	B	G. G. Harrap and Co.	1944

Type	No. of forms	C.A. range	Skills tested	Time
Group, attainment			Vocabulary tests:	
Group, attainment	I	10 : 0 to 15 : 0	1. One hundred common names	50′
Group, attainment	I	10 : 0 to 15 : 0	2. One hundred common class names	50′
Group, attainment	I	10 : 0 to 15 : 0	3. One hundred common verbs	50′
Group, attainment	I	10 : 0 to 15 : 0	4. One hundred common adjectives (List A)	50′
Group, attainment	I	10 : 0 to 15 : 0	5. One hundred common adjectives (List B)	50′
Individual, oral	I	4 : 3 to 8 : 3	6. A vocabulary test for young children	Untimed
Group, attainment	I	11 : 0 to 15 : 0	7. Words with more than one meaning	Untimed
Group, attainment	I	11 : 0 to 15 : 0	8. Ideational addition	Untimed
Group, attainment	I	10 : 0 to 13 : 0	1. A sentence completion test	Untimed
Individual, oral	I	4 : 0 to 10 : 0	2. An English language scale	Untimed
Group, attainment	I	8 : 0 to 12 : 0	3. Sentence patterns	Untimed
Group, attainment	I	8 : 3 to 10 : 8	4. Connecting words and phrases	40′
Group, attainment	I	8 : 6 to 11 : 6	5. A reported speech test	Untimed
Group, attainment	I	6 : 6 to 11 : 0	1. Sentences for a reading scale	Untimed
Group, attainment	I	7 : 0 to 11 : 0	2. Questions on the reading scale for infants and juniors (reading comprehension)	Untimed
Group, attainment	I	11 : 0 to 15 : 0	3. Reading tests for seniors	Untimed
Group, attainment	I	9 : 0 to 14 : 0	4. Sentence-arrangement tests	Untimed
Group, attainment		10 : 0 to 15 : 0	5. Time-relation tests:	
Group, attainment	I		(*a*) Related actions	Untimed
Group, attainment	I		(*b*) Common time relation words	Untimed
Group, attainment	I	10 : 0 to 14 : 0	6. (1) Paired qualities test	Untimed
			(2) An Aesop's Fables Test for older children	Untimed
(level A)				

Comments: These tests are contained in Watts, A. F. (1957) *The Language and Mental Development of Children*, 6th reprint. Despite their technical limitations by today's standards, within Watts' tests are some excellent ideas worthy of development.

TRN	Name of test	Author	Country	Publisher	Year
87	*Wide-Span Reading Test*	M. A. Brimer and H. Gross	B	Nelson	1972

Type	No. of forms	C.A. range	Skills tested	Time
Group, attainment and diagnostic	2 (A & B)	7 : 0 to 15 : 0	*Attainment* 1. Silent reading comprehension *Diagnostic indicators* 1. Decoding 2. Linguistic	30′
(level A)			3. Vocabulary	

Comments: This eighty-item test in reusable booklet form asks the child to complete a sentence having one word missing. The word to be entered is selected from another sentence to the left of the incomplete one. Responses are recorded on separate answer sheets.

e.g. A. Clear the table and wash up the dishes.

                We   with soap and water.

The test is arranged in eight levels, four each for the junior and secondary schools respectively. The standardisation claims to be on a sample of children in schools representative of the national distribution of schools. Test-retest reliabilities are satisfactory. No data are presented concerning validities. The Diagnostic Indicators are 'valid' only if there are at least ten incorrect responses within the range given, presumably in a given diagnostic indicator category. A number of important qualifications are made concerning the use of this part of the test. This seems the least valuable part of the test to the reviewer. Whether it is desirable to use only eighty items to cover such a wide age and ability range is a point which the test user must decide in the light of his purposes in testing reading.

TRN	Name of test		Author		Country	Publisher		Year
91	*Word Recognition Test*		C. Carver		B	Hodder and Stoughton Educational		1970

Type	No. of forms	C.A. range	Skills tested		Time
Group or individual, attainment and diagnostic, multiple-choice	1	4 : 6 to 8 : 6	Word recognition Patterns of errors (a) Initial letters (b) Mid vowel sounds (c) Distortions of letters (d) Distortions of words (e) Reversals (f) Word endings	(g) Initial multiple consonants (h) Combined vowels (i) Sight/regular words (j) Other errors	Untimed (15'-30')
(level A)					

Comments: This test, developed by an experienced remedial teacher in the Manchester area whilst taking an advanced course of study in Educational Guidance at the University, contains fifty items. Each item consists of a row of five or six words, only one of which is the correct answer. The teacher gives the stimulus word orally in a sentence specified in the manual. The child underlines the word he believes the tester has spoken. Raw scores are converted to reading ages and Word Recognition Ability levels. Sex differences in the skills tested are ignored. The test is intended to assess the early stages of word recognition and to provide the opportunity for the analysis of individual error patterns. Carver claims that the test can be used with four to five-year-old children in small groups. For children who are clearly non-readers in the sense that they cannot cope with any of the first ten items, an alternative activity is allowed for in the test booklet. According to Carver, the test reveals both the child's knowledge of the visual presentation of sounds and words, and also the child's ability to analyse sounds themselves. The aural analysis of words is considered a crucial pre-requisite for word recognition and the alternatives in the multiple-choice are 'systematic and structured alternatives' to the correct answer.

The manual provides a brief analysis of ten stages in word recognition ability ranging from the level of virtually no knowledge to that appropriate to a word recognition ability level of about 8 : 6. The original sample on which the items were tested was a very small one and the work was carried out in 1962. However, the evidence in the manual indicates that the test is both reliable and valid.

This test has been used extensively for screening purposes in the Manchester area. Its use with individual children as a source of diagnostic information is less popular, possibly because of the time required.

(b) *Others*

TRN	Name of test	Author	Country	Publisher	Year
5	*ACER Primary Reading Survey Tests A-D*	Australian Council for Educational Research	A	Australian Council for Educational Research	1972

Type	No. of forms	C.A. range	Skills tested		Time
Group, attainment	1 (R)	8:0 to 9:0	A.	Word knowledge (40 items, multiple-choice synonyms)	20′
	2 (R & S)			Comprehension (35 items, multiple-choice)	30′
	1 (R)	9:0 to 10:0	B.	Word knowledge (45 items, multiple-choice, synonyms)	20′
	2 (R & S)			Comprehension (38 items, multiple-choice)	30′
	1 (R)	10:0 to 11:0	C.	Word knowledge (45 items, multiple-choice, synonyms)	20′
	2 (R & S)			Comprehension (39 items, multiple-choice)	30′
	1 (R)	11:0 to 12:0	D.	Word knowledge (40 items, multiple-choice, synonyms)	20′
(level A)				Comprehension (34 items, multiple-choice)	30′

Comments: This series of reading tests is designed to assess two aspects of the reading skills of primary school pupils. Standardisation is based on representative samples of Australian children. The need for the compilation of local and state norms is stressed. The tests have high reliabilities and validities. Because the final form of the test manual is still in preparation, pertinent technical information can be obtained from the Advisory Services of the ACER.

This information will be included in the final manual for the tests.

TRN	Name of Test		Author	Country	Publisher		Year
7	*Basic Sight Word Test*		E. W. Dolch	USA	Garrard Publishing Co.		1942

Type	No. of forms	C.A. range	Skills tested		Time
Group or individual mastery test	1	Mainly primary school, but also poor readers at any age	Word recognition		Untimed (4 × 15′ sessions)

(level A)

Comments: This word recognition test presents the complete Basic Sight Vocabulary, comprising the 220 words which are the content of 70 per cent of first readers and up to 65 per cent of second and third readers in graded reading series.

Dolch argues that competent reading requires that the child be able to recognise these 220 words immediately on sight if he is to become an effective reader. Thus the test is a 'mastery' test of a particularly important content.

No norms are given for the test, the raw score of words correct being seen as a valid index of the child's mastery of the skill tested. The aim is for all children to master all of these words as soon as possible, consistent with individual differences. There are numerous English Word Lists which teachers can adapt to act as 'mastery' tests.

TRN	Name of test	Author	Country	Publisher	Year
8	*Botel Reading Inventory*	M. Botel, C. Holsclaw, G. Cammarota and R. K. Flamond	USA	Follet Publishing Co.	1966

Type	No. of forms	C.A. range	Skills tested	Time
Group and individual, content criterion-referenced	6 (A & B) (A & B)	7 : 0 to 12 : +	1. Phonics mastery test 2. Word recognition test	Untimed
(level A)	(A & B)		3. Word opposites test (comprehension)	

Comments: On the assumption that 'standardised testing methods have not been successful in determining proper placement' of pupils to levels of reading books, Botel claims to have capitalised on the informal testing procedures used by effective reading teachers. His tests are content criterion-referenced. The results are interpreted in terms of the children's levels of mastery of the skills tested.

No evidence of reliabilities or validities is given, nor is the content the tests sample clearly specified. The tests appear to be based on Botel's analysis of the skills comprising the reading process. Whilst his ideas may be valid, and whilst content criterion-referenced measurement and testing is important in the assessment of reading, to use the *Inventory* is, on the evidence presented, an act of faith in Botel's claims.

TRN	Name of test	Author	Country	Publisher	Year
9	*Brief Test of Literacy*	T. F. Donlon, W. M. McPeek and L. R. Chatham	USA	US Department of Health, Education and Welfare	1968

Type	No. of forms	C.A. range	Skills tested	Time
Group, attainment	1	10 : 0+	1. Reading comprehension	Untimed
			2. Writing dictated sentences	(7′)
(level A)				

Comments: As part of a National Health Survey, this test was designed to produce two scores, each giving a classification of 'literate' or not. The reading test required a reading performance equivalent to that of the average ten-year-old as a criterion of literacy. It contains seven paragraphs each with three five-option multiple-choice questions. The writing test requires the subject to record five dictated sentences which were scored for errors. One minute is allowed for each sentence to be written. Thus it is a form of timed spelling test. If the subject scores differently on the two parts of the test, the reading test result is to be taken as the better indicator. The test has satisfactory reliabilities and concurrent validities, although the standardisation sample was rather limited. Work has been done in England on this test at the University of Manchester Department of Education.

TRN	Name of test	Author	Country	Publisher	Year
12	*California Phonics Survey*	G. M. Brown and A. B. Cottrell	USA	California Test Bureau	1956 to 1963

Type	No. of forms	C.A. range	Skills tested	Time
Group, diagnostic	2 (1 & 2) (Form 2 only gives Total Score)	13 : 0 to 18 : 0	1. Long-short vowel confusion 2. Other vowel confusion 3. Consonants confusion with blends and digraphs 4. Consonant-vowel reversals 5. Configurations 6. Endings 7. Negatives—opposites—sight words 8. Rigidity 9. Total	40'-45'
(level A)				

Comments: This seventy-five-item test, which has tape-recorded instructions as an alternative to the use of a manual, is divided into five units, each of which includes items of different types measuring various phonic skills. Individual responses are analysed and plotted on a profile sheet. This provides a basis for diagnosis and remedial prescription. The standard error of measurement is utilised to determine the points dividing students whose phonic skills are adequate from those who have difficulties.

The items were selected so as to include all of the commonly used speech sounds in their normal spelling.

The seventh revision of this test was used in a national standardisation programme at various age levels to obtain the information on reliabilities and validities which is presented.

This appears a promising test for use in secondary and tertiary education where mastery of phonic skills is suspect.

TRN	Name of test	Author	Country	Publisher	Year
16	*Diagnostic Reading Tests*	Committee on Diagnostic Reading Tests	USA	Committee on Diagnostic Reading Tests, Inc. (Science Research Associates act as agents for some parts)	1947 to 1966

Type	No. of forms	C.A. range	Skills tested	Time
Diagnostic, group and individual (level A)	There are many forms at various levels	5 : 0 to 18 : 0	Almost every skill a teacher might consider important in reading is tested in one or another of the three batteries	

Comments: This is the most comprehensive single attempt to produce an all-embracing series of diagnostic tests. These tests are made up of three batteries, covering ages five to nine, nine to thirteen and twelve to eighteen years respectively. Each battery includes a survey test intended to assess the pupil's general reading proficiency, plus a host of supplementary tests, indeed so many that the interested reader must obtain further details from Buros or from the Committee.

The laudable aim of the Committee was to produce tests that could be scored in areas of reading instruction rather than in terms of 'pure factors'. Teachers of reading were consulted right from the start of the project. Of the three batteries, the first appears to be the least valuable. The production of the material that the reviewer has inspected is of variable quality, but the scope of the series is awe-inspiring. This does not necessarily mean that the tests are the best available for the diagnosis of reading failure. Nonetheless, the series is one of which teachers should be aware. A similar project in the UK might find considerable support from the educational world.

H

TRN	Name of test	Author	Country	Publisher	Year
18	*Doren Diagnostic Reading Test of Word Recognition Skills*	M. Doren	USA	American Guidance Service, Inc. (Educational Enterprises, Bristol, act as agents)	1956 to 1964

Type	No. of forms	C.A. range	Skills tested		Time
Group, diagnostic	1	6 : 0 to 15 : 0	1. Letter recognition	7. Blending	3 × 60' sessions
			2. Beginning sounds	8. Rhyming	
			3. Whole-word recognition	9. Vowels	
			4. Words within words	10. Sight words	
			5. Speech consonants	11. Discriminate guessing	
(level A)			6. Ending sounds	12. Total	

(Each of the sub-tests 1 to 11 comprises two or more sections)

Comments: The content of the eleven sub-tests is based on an analysis of the word recognition skills required to cope with the initial three books in five extensively-used series of graded readers. Doren's stated purpose is to identify the students' mistakes, thus specifying the skills towards which remedial work might profitably be directed. The reliability coefficients of the sub-tests range from 0·53 to 0·88, thus great care is required in interpreting the profiles. A concurrent validity coefficient of 0·90 for total score with reading attainment in the first four school grades is given. Validity coefficients for each grade level range from 0·77 to 0·92. Some of the sub-test items appear suspect; for example, 'Beginning Sounds', at some levels, seems to tap skills requiring the use of context and of sight vocabulary as much as the skill it purports to measure.

Suggestions for remedial activities are given. These appear to be based on sound teaching principles, but no evidence is given of the efficacy of the practices with children having particular difficulties.

TRN 20	Name of test *Durrell Analysis of Reading Difficulty*	Author D. D. Durrell	Country USA	Publisher Harcourt, Brace and World, Inc. (NFER act as agents)	Year 1937 to 1955

Type Individual, diagnostic	No. of forms I	C.A. range Pre-reading to 12 : 0	Skills tested	Time 30'-90'

Skills tested

Pre-primer level
1. Visual memory of word forms
2. Auditory analysis of word elements
3. Letter recognition
4. Phonics
5. Learning rate
6. Listening comprehension

Primer level
1. Oral reading (comprehension, reading errors, speed)
2. Silent reading (recall, mechanics of reading)
3. Listening test (comprehension)
4. Word recognition and analysis (use of tachistoscope)
5. Supplementary test of written spelling, and speed of handwriting
6. Suggestions for informal tests of suitability of textbooks for instruction, evaluating study abilities, speed of reading, reading interest and effort

(level P)

Comments: The primary aim of this test is to specify weaknesses and faulty habits which may then be corrected. The standardisation data are meagre, thereby making difficult the interpretation of normative scores, where these are given. The reliabilities, validities and inter-correlations of the sub-tests are not given. Hence the interpretation of profiles is made doubly difficult. On the positive side, the major value of the analysis is the incorporated checklists for the observation of various reading skills. These checklists are very detailed. As the author says: 'The checklists for recording observations of difficulties are the most important feature of the Analysis. While norms are provided for many of the tests, a record of the difficulties the child displays is more important than the level of attainment. The items on the checklists are those of highest frequency and significance in remedial work.' In one sense, the non-normative use of checklists is an approach to mastery testing or criterion-referenced testing. The checklists are likely to be of value to the experienced teacher of reading, but it is a pity that the tests to which they are related have not a more adequate psychometric pedigree. The administration and interpretation of the test requires an appropriate course of training and a considerable amount of practice.

TRN	Name of test	Author	Country	Publisher	Year
21	*Durrell Listening-Reading Series*	D. D. Durrell	USA	Harcourt, Brace and Jovanovich, Inc.	1970 (Primary, Intermediate) and 1969 (Advanced)

Type	No. of forms	C.A. range	Skills tested	Time
Group or individual, diagnostic and attainment	2 (D & E) Primary	6 : 0 to 9 : 6	1. Vocabulary (listening comprehension)	20′
			2. Sentence (listening comprehension)	15′
			3. Vocabulary (reading comprehension)	20′
			4. Sentence (reading comprehension)	15′
	2 (D & E) Intermediate	9 : 6 to 12 : 0	1. Vocabulary (listening comprehension)	20′
			2. Paragraph (listening comprehension)	23′
			3. Vocabulary (reading comprehension)	20′
			4. Paragraph (reading comprehension)	23′
	2 (D & E) Advanced	13 : 0 to 16 : 0	1. Vocabulary (listening comprehension)	20′
			2. Paragraph (listening comprehension)	20′
			3. Vocabulary (reading comprehension)	20′
(level P)			4. Paragraph (reading comprehension)	20′

Comments: The aim of these tests is to compare the child's understanding of equivalent material presented orally and requiring no reading attainments, with his ability to read and understand. In one part of the test he listens and responds whereas in the other section he reads and responds. The manual presents details of an extensive standardisation programme and also gives evidence of satisfactory reliabilities and validities. Intercorrelations between parts of the tests and correlations with other tests are presented. The authors argue that listening comprehension is a most satisfactory measure of a child's 'potential' for reading. However, it is also noted that some children's reading scores exceed their listening scores. Thus whilst listening scores indicate the extent to which a child can understand spoken language, it is not necessarily the level at which the child *should* be reading. Neither does it set an upper limit to reading attainment: 'Actually, a higher score in either of these abilities indicates a "potential" level for the other' (Primary manual, p. 16). Whilst care has been taken to make the content of listening and reading tests equivalent though different, one could see interpretation being easier in some respects if the material was identical but the order different. The interpretation of the differences between scores on the listening and reading tests requires some sophistication, but is within the capabilities of any interested teacher. The manual contains helpful comments on the translation of results into remedial programmes.

This test is a most interesting approach to differential diagnosis.

TRN 29	Name of test *Gates-McKillop Reading Diagnostic Tests*	Author A. I. Gates and A. S. McKillop	Country USA	Publisher Teachers College Press, New York	Year 1926 to 1962

Type Diagnostic, individual	No. of forms 2 (1 & 2)	C.A. range 8 : 0 to 12 : 0	Skills tested	Time 30'-60'
			Sub-test	
			1. Oral reading test scored for 11 types of error	
			2. Words (Flash presentation)	
			3. Words (Untimed)	
			4. Phrases (Flash presentation)	
			5. Knowledge of word parts:	
			(a) recognising and blending common word parts	
			(b) giving letter sounds	
			(c) naming capital letters	
			(d) naming lower case letters	
			6. Recognising the visual form of word equivalents of sounds (4 scores)	
			7. Auditory blending	
			8. (a) Oral spelling of words	
			(b) Oral vocabulary	
(level P)			(c) Syllabication	
			(d) Auditory discrimination	

Comments: This extensive diagnostic test provides a detailed profile of a child's reading skills, consisting of twenty-eight scores. The most noticeable omission is that of a test of reading comprehension. The tests are generally simple to administer and score. The dangers of over-interpreting the differences between scores in the diagnostic profile are stressed, but as insufficient information concerning sub-test reliabilities and intercorrelations is given, much of the interpretation of the profiles must be clinical. The suggestions for profile analysis that are given in the manual appear to be of value, but evidence of their efficacy is lacking.

TRN 30	Name of test *Gates-MacGinitie Reading Test*	Author A. I. Gates and W. H. MacGinitie	Country USA	Publisher Teachers College Press (NFER act as agents)	Year 1965 (Grades 1-9) 1969 (Grades 10-12)

Type Group, attainment	No. of forms	C.A. range	Skills tested	Time
	1 & 2	7 : 0	Grade 1. Vocabulary and Comprehension (Primary A)	15′ & 25′
	1 & 2	8 : 0	Grade 2. Vocabulary and Comprehension (Primary B)	15′ & 25′
	1 & 2	9 : 0	Grade 3. Vocabulary and Comprehension (Primary C)	20′ & 30′
	1, 2 & 3	8 : 0 to 9 : 0	Grades 2-3. Speed and Accuracy (Primary CS)	7′
	1, 2 & 3	10 : 0 to 12 : 0	Grades 4-6. Speed and Accuracy, Vocabulary and Comprehension (Survey D)	5′, 15′, 25′
	1, 2 & 3	13 : 0 to 15 : 0	Grades 7-9. Speed and Accuracy, Vocabulary and Comprehension (Survey E)	4′, 15′, 25′
(level A)	1 & 2	16 : 0 to 18 : 0	Grades 10-12. Speed and Accuracy, Vocabulary and Comprehension (Survey F)	4′, 15′, 25′

Comments: This is an example of a series of reading tests devised to form an effective testing programme for measuring group and individual reading attainments throughout a child's school career. Norms are based on a large-scale standardisation in 1965. The technical supplements to the test manuals provide evidence of reliabilities and validities.

Certain of the above tests are available in both hand- and machine-scoring format.

This particular series is included as the NFER has recently begun collecting data on English children's performance on an anglicised version of Primary A Form 1.

TRN	Name of test	Author	Country	Publisher	Year
35	*Gilmore Oral Reading Test*	J. V. Gilmore and E. C. Gilmore	USA	Harcourt, Brace and World, Inc.	1968

Type	No. of forms	C.A. range	Skills tested	Time
Individual, oral, diagnostic	4 (A, B, C & D)	6 : 0 to 14 : 0	*Oral reading* (*a*) accuracy (*b*) comprehension (*c*) rate of reading *Error analysis* substitutions, mispronunciations, words pronounced by examiner, disregard of punctuation, insertions, hesitations, repetitions, omissions, total errors	15'-20'

(level A)

Comments: The test comprises ten paragraphs, arranged in order of difficulty, which form a continuous story. Five comprehension questions are asked at the end of each paragraph. Norms for accuracy, comprehension and rate of reading are provided in terms of 'grade equivalents'. During the test, an analysis is made of the child's errors as the prime purpose of the test is an analysis of oral reading skills. Some limited guidance is given on the interpretation of the three main results.

However, the interpretation of the patterns of error scores is not adequately discussed. The standardisation, reliabilities and validities of the test are reported. As might be expected, the small number of items per year in the comprehension scale reduces its parallel form reliability for a given year grade. Accuracy and Rate are more reliably measured.

The test is an interesting one because the variables of sentence length and percentage of complex sentences were controlled in its construction.

TRN 38	Name of test *Gray Oral Reading Test*	Author W. S. Gray and H. M. Robinson	Country USA	Publisher Bobbs-Merrill Co., Inc.	Year 1963 to 1967

Type Individual, attainment and diagnostic	No. of forms 4 (A, B, C & D)	C.A. range 6 : 0 to 18 : 0	Skills tested 1. Oral reading achievement 2. Types of errors (a) aid (b) gross mispronunciation (c) partial mispronunciation (d) omission (e) insertion (f) substitution (g) repetition (h) inversion	Time The time taken to read a passage is measured

(level P)

Comments: These tests are designed to measure oral reading using thirteen passages of increasing complexity ranging from pre-primer to college level, although it is difficult for beginning readers. It is claimed that the results of the test will provide a quick and valid means of placing a child at a level of work suited to his reading skills. The standardisation and norms are based on rather small and restricted samples. Separate norms for boys and girls are provided. The standard error of measurement of the tests increases markedly as the more advanced levels are reached. Nonetheless, the test compares favourably with other oral tests of reading. Claims for the test's validity are based on its construction and content. The availability of four equivalent forms is a considerable asset.

TRN	Name of test	Author	Country	Publisher	Year
46	*Inventory-Survey Test* (standardised edition)	M. Monroe	USA	Scott, Foresman & Company	1968 (Intermediate) and 1969 (Primary and Advanced)

Type	No. of forms	C.A. range	Skills tested	Time
Group attainment	2 (A & B) (Primary)	8 : 0 to 10 : 0	I. Comprehension: (*a*) word and phrase meaning (*b*) Sentence meaning (*c*) paragraph meaning II. Word analysis: (*a*) scrutiny (*b*) phoneme-grapheme relationship (*c*) inflection and derivation	Untimed
	2 (A & B) (Intermediate)	10 : 0 to 13 : 0	I. Word meaning II. Sentence meaning III. Paragraph meaning IV. Word analysis V. Dictionary skills	
(level A)	2 (A & B) (Advanced)	13 : 0 to 15 : 0	(Skills tested as for the Intermediate level)	

Comments: This series of tests, constructed by one of the most eminent workers in this field, is designed to measure a pupil's general level of reading attainment. The areas sampled are such that examination of the profiles of a child will suggest ways in which help for the individual can be provided. The standardisation samples for the three levels of the test are clearly specified and the split-half reliabilities of the tests are 0·93, 0·92 and 0·96 respectively. Raw scores can be converted to standard scores and percentile ranks. No evidence on validities is presented and neither the reliabilities of the sub-tests nor their intercorrelations are reported. The advice given on interpreting the profile scores is clearly explained, albeit at a relatively rule-of-thumb level.

TRN	Name of test	Author	Country	Publisher	Year
50	*Marino Graded Word Reading Scale*	J. Sullivan	E	Longman, Browne & Nolan, Dublin	1970

Type	No. of forms	C.A. range	Skills tested		Time
Attainment, individual, oral	1	5 : 0 to 15 : 0	Oral word reading		Untimed (10')
(level A)					

Comments: This is a 130-item word recognition test. It is intended for the age range 7+ to 12+ years in particular. However, reading ages can be obtained, ranging from a base of five years (no words read correctly) to twenty years (130 words read correctly). The extremes of the scale are likely to be suspect, especially the upper end.

The test was standardised on a sample of 3930 children aged between five and fifteen years. Raw scores can be converted to reading ages only and this would be considered a weakness by some test constructors.

The manual is clearly written and provides satisfactory evidence of validities and reliabilities. The account of the test construction procedure given in the appendix to the manual manages to combine brevity with lucidity.

It is highly likely that this test will become very popular in Eire and may well find uses in Great Britain after some comparative investigations have been carried out.

TRN	Name of test	Author	Country	Publisher	Year
51	*Mastery Test* * (1)	E. R. Sipay	USA	Cassell Collier-Macmillan Ltd, London	1969 to 1970

Type	No. of forms	C.A. range	Skills tested	Time
Group, content criterion-referenced (level A)	1	Pre-primer	1. Word recognition (30 items) 2. Word analysis (25 items) 3. Comprehension (20 items) 4. Total (75 items)	Untimed

Comments: This is the first of a series of tests designed to discover whether the child has mastered the reading skills taught at the pre-primer reader level. As the tests have been designed to sample *only* the skills in which instruction has been given, children's scores can be expected to cluster at the top end of the scale. This contrasts with normative tests in which children's scores are more normally distributed. The pattern of a child's scores on the sub-tests indicates the effectiveness of the instructional programme for him. Mastery tests, such as the above, sample specific skills in greater detail than most normative tests. The child's scores are expressed as percentage correct and their achievement rated 'Excellent', 'Good', 'Doubtful' and 'Unsatisfactory'. For example, in Word Recognition, any score *less than 90 per cent* is interpreted as showing that the child needs extra help. The test constructor has apparently used conventional indices of validities and reliabilities as calculated for normative tests to describe the test characteristics. Almost inevitably, this results in some apparently low sub-test reliabilities. This is to be expected when what is not the most appropriate statistic is used. Better indices are being developed. As the test is supposed to sample the skills developed by the reading programme, the content validity of the test is readily controlled and appears to be high.

* These tests have been devised for *each* book in the reading programme for Primary Grades written by A. J. Harris and M. K. Clark and known as *The Macmillan Reading Programme*. The two examples given are of the first and final tests in the series.

TRN	Name of test	Author	Country	Publisher	Year
52	*Mastery Test* (2)	E. R. Sipay	USA	Cassell Collier-Macmillan Ltd, London	1968 to 1970

Type	No. of forms	C.A. range	Skills tested	Time

Group, content criterion-referenced	1	Test for 3rd readers	1. Word recognition (25 items)
			2. Word analysis (60 items)
			   (*a*) consonants
			   (*b*) vowels
			   (*c*) plurals, prefixes, suffixes, homonyms
			   (*d*) silent letters
			   (*e*) syllabification
			   (*f*) accent
			3. Comprehension (40 items)
			   (*a*) main ideas
			   (*b*) stated facts
			   (*c*) inferences
			   (*d*) vocabulary
				Untimed

(level A)

Comments: This test is designed to measure the extent to which a child has mastered the reading skills taught at a given level. As with *Mastery Test* (1), it is a content criterion-referenced test. The comment made concerning that test also applies to this one in terms of validities and reliabilities.

In terms of the skills tested, the considerable extension from *Mastery Test* (1) can be seen. There are a further five intermediate readers and *Mastery Tests* linked to them. The content of any series of mastery tests of reading constitutes the component skills of reading.

TRN	Name of test	Author		Country	Publisher		Year
53	*McCullough Word-Analysis Tests*	C. M. McCullough		USA	Personnel Press, Inc.		1960 to 1963

Type	No. of forms	C.A. range	Skills tested	Time
Group or individual, diagnostic and attainment	1	9 : 0 to 11 : 0	*Phonetic* 1. Consonants: initial blends and digraphs 2. Vowel sounds: phonetic discriminations 3. Vowels: matching letters to vowel sounds 4. Sounding whole words 5. Interpreting phonetic symbols *Structural* 6. Dividing words into syllables 7. Root words in affixed form 8. Total for 1-5 9. Total for 6 and 7 10. Total for all tests	Untimed (7 × 10' sessions)
(level P)				

Comments: The first three of the seven sub-tests of this battery assess the child's ability to decode aurally-received information. The other four tests are silent ones. The sub-tests have generally acceptably high internal consistency reliabilities (for the three grade levels covered in the seven sub-tests these range from 0·76 to 0·97). There is an excellent individual record booklet which facilitates the inter-relationship of information from the sub-tests. Despite limitations in the description of the standardisation procedure, the tests are one of the better instruments available for assessing mechanical aspects of word-analysis and for the diagnosis of failure. The manual is very helpful in the interpretation of the test scores. Such a test battery can help to improve the focus of remedial teaching.

TRN	Name of test	Author	Country	Publisher	Year
65	*Nelson-Denny Reading Test* (revised edition)	M. J. Nelson, E. C. Denny and J. I. Brown	USA	Houghton-Mifflin, Co. (NFER act as agents)	1960

Type	No. of forms	C.A. range	Skills tested	Time
Group, attainment and diagnostic (level A)	2 (A & B)	15 : 0 to 18 : 0 (and adult)	Vocabulary (100 multiple-choice items) Comprehension (36 multiple-choice items) Rate	30′-35′

Comments: This is a valuable test for use with able upper school and college students. The suggestion that reductions in the administration times allows the test to be extended for use with adults, is suspect. Otherwise, the standardisation of the test is sound, being based on an American sample selected on the basis of school size by region and community size within region. Reliabilities and validities are appropriately high.

The material in the test appears too difficult for the average fifteen to sixteen-year-old pupil.

The test has been used to evaluate adults' improvements after taking courses in 'efficient reading'.

The manual is not particularly helpful in making suggestions as to how the scores can be related to the improvement of the skills measured.

TRN	Name of test	Author		Country	Publisher	Year
67a	*Prescriptive Reading Inventory* (hereafter PRI)	CTB/McGraw-Hill Authorship Staff		USA	CTB/McGraw-Hill	1972, 1974

Type	No. of forms	C.A. range	Skills tested	Time
Group and individual, diagnostic, criterion-referenced	4 A B C D	7:6 to 8:6 8:0 to 9:6 9:0 to 10:6 10:0 to 12:0	The reading behaviour expected from prescribed instruction is defined in terms of 90 objectives. These objectives are grouped under the following processes: 1. Recognition of sound and symbol 2. Phonic analysis 3. Structural analysis 4. Translation 5. Literal comprehension 6. Interpretive comprehension 7. Critical comprehension	Untimed (3½ hrs) (3 hrs) (3 hrs) (2¾ hrs)

(level A)

Comments: The PRI is designed to allow the diagnostic teaching of reading based on ninety clearly defined objectives. The analysis of the results is directly linked to the prescription of appropriate reading activities likely to develop the skills that have not been mastered. Currently the PRI is keyed to thirty-two reading schemes. This number is being increased. Although the PRI can be scored by hand, the process is very time-consuming. A computer scoring system is provided by CTB/McGraw-Hill at a low cost. The service provides the following information for the teacher:

1. *Individual Diagnostic Map.* This specifies the objectives that a pupil has mastered, needs to review, or has been unable to cope with.
2. *Class Diagnostic Map.* This summarises the results on each objective tested for a class.
3. *Class Grouping Report.* This identifies the reading skill weaknesses within a class on the objectives tested at that level.

4. *Objective Mastery Report.* Provides an overall picture of how well a class has mastered the appropriate PRI objectives.
5. *Individual Study Guide.* Identifies each individual child's reading strengths and weaknesses and provides an educational prescription linked to the reading programme in use in the school.
6. *Interpretative Handbook.* This lists the objectives measured, explains how the previous reports can be interpreted and suggests remedial activities.

The scope and promise of the PRI is extremely impressive. It will be interesting to receive reports of the efficacy with which its use alleviates children's reading difficulties and raises standards of literacy. It should be noted that within the system there is still considerable scope for the teacher's ingenuity in devising remedial materials and techniques.

TRN	Name of test	Author	Country	Publisher	Year
69	*Progressive Achievement Tests: Listening Comprehension*	W. B. Elley and N. A. Reid	NZ	New Zealand Council for Educational Research	1971

Type	No. of forms	C.A. range	Skills tested	Time
Oral, group, attainment and diagnostic	2 (A & B at each of the eight levels)	7 : 0 to 15 : 0	Listening comprehension	Times in which tester must read passages are prescribed
(level A)				

Comments: In this test the teacher reads passages, related questions and four alternative answers after each question. The child's task is to select the correct answer from those read aloud. His response is recorded by a letter, i.e. A, B, C or D. Like the *Progressive Achievement Tests of Reading Comprehension and Vocabulary*, this test is intended to be used early in the school year in order to give information helpful to the teacher in planning a programme of instruction.

Standardisation is based on representative samples of 1000 pupils at each age level. Reliabilities and validities are acceptably high. The manual is excellent. Raw scores are converted to percentiles for each six months of age range covered. One possible weakness is that there are relatively few test items per level or year.

The uses of a listening comprehension test to provide an estimate of a child's 'reading expectancy' is interestingly and cautiously discussed. Teachers in New Zealand are fortunate to have the series of *Progressive Achievement Tests* available to them.

TRN	Name of test	Author	Country	Publisher	Year
70	*Progressive Achievement Tests: Reading Comprehension and Vocabulary*	W. B. Elley and N. A. Reid	NZ	New Zealand Council for Educational Research (Hodder and Stoughton Educational act as agents)	1969

Type	No. of forms	C.A. range	Skills tested	Time
Group, attainment	3 (A, B & C)	8 : 0 to 15 : 0	Vocabulary (125 items)	30'
			Reading comprehension (97 items)	40'
(level A)			(A series of 7 sub-tests of these scales appropriate to particular age levels of pupils has been prepared)	

Comments: This series of seven tests is designed to enable teachers to assess their pupils' levels of achievement in terms of a reading content and of reading objectives measured by the tests. In the vocabulary tests, the underlying content scale is based on the most frequently known 10 000 words in the English language, according to the Wright* (1965) list. Scores are recorded in ten levels and equivalent average ages of children performing at that level for both the vocabulary and comprehension tests are given. Thus the test gives both a content mastery score and a percentile rank for each six-month age group from 8 : 0 to 15 : 0, if required. The level scores place a child's reading attainments on a ten-stage developmental scale ranging from illiteracy to the competence of the adult.

The test is available in three parallel forms, A, B and C, but the C form is reserved for research purposes only. The reusable test booklets contain the complete test in either vocabulary or comprehension for Forms A, B or C and the separate answer sheets are prepared for *each* of the seven sub-sections of the scale. The split-half reliabilities and the equivalent form correlations for both aspects of reading tested are satisfactory. Evidence of concurrent validities is also presented. Content validity is clearly defined. The handbook contains extremely helpful suggestions on the use of reading tests and the interpretation of the results. One weakness is that the uses of the tests as indicators of mastery of content criteria depend on rather few items for each level of achievement. On balance, this is a well-designed and well-constructed test with a most useful manual describing what any test user needs to know.

A set of *Listening Comprehension Tests* have also been developed to be used in conjunction with the above reading tests so that some indication of level of expectancy in reading attainment by a child can be estimated by the teacher.

*Wright, C. W. (1965) *An English Word Count*. Pretoria, South Africa: National Bureau of Educational and Social Research.

I

TRN	Name of test	Author	Country	Publisher	Year
73	*Reading Versatility Tests*	A. S. McDonald, Sr. M. Alodia, G. Zimny and J. Byrne	USA	Educational Development Laboratories	1962 to 1968

Type	No. of forms	C.A. range	Skills tested		Time
Group and individual, diagnostic	4 (A, B, C, D) (Basic)*	11:0 to 14:0	1.	(a) Rate of reading (fiction)	40'-50'
				(b) Comprehension	
			2.	(a) Rate of reading (non-fiction)	
				(b) Comprehension	
	4 (A, B, C, D) (Intermediate)	14:0 to 18:0	3.	(a) Rate of skimming	
				(b) Comprehension—search for main ideas	
	4 (A, B, C, D) (Advanced)	18:0+	4.	(a) Rate of scanning	
(level P)				(b) Comprehension—answering a question asked in advance	

Comments: This series of tests at three levels takes the form of a number of passages of reading of different types, i.e. fiction and non-fiction, and determines the student's ability to read for different purposes such as skimming and scanning. The authors claim that the test enables the teacher to see under what conditions and with which materials the student reads effectively. It also points to the student's efficiency and versatility. The timing of the passages is central to the marking of the test and a 'Test-Timer' is provided so that individuals can record times taken by themselves in completing prescribed sections of the test.

Details of test construction and standardisation are not given, but some partial evidence of reliabilities and validities is reported. The

interpretation of the results is described, but is quite complex. Comprehension scores of below 60 per cent correct invalidates the other results. The main concern of the test appears to be non-normative comparison of intra-individual differences in a student's reading of various materials for various purposes.

At present, this test appears to have considerable promise, but further technical information concerning its characteristics and validities would improve the chances of its being used effectively.

* There is a second part to the Basic Test intended for Grades 6–10 which requires the use of an eye-movement camera.

TRN	Name of test	Author	Country	Publisher	Year
80	*Stanford Diagnostic Reading Test*	B. Karlsen, R. Madden and E. F. Gardner	USA	Harcourt, Brace and World, Inc.	1966

Type	No. of forms	C.A. range	Skills tested	Time
Group or individual, diagnostic	2 (W & X)	8 : 0 to 10 : 0	1. Reading comprehension 2. Vocabulary 3. Auditory discrimination 4. Syllabication 5. Beginning and ending sounds 6. Blending 7. Sound discrimination	4 sessions totalling 2¾ hrs
(level A)	2 (W & X)	10 : 0 to 14 : 0	1. Reading comprehension (literal and inferential) 2. Vocabulary 3. Syllabication 4. Sound discrimination 5. Blending 6. Rate of reading	

Comments: These tests are designed for use by classroom teachers and the interpretation of the results is related to classroom reading instruction. The tests also have value in a clinical setting. They are based on the authors' analysis of over 200 studies concerning the nature of the reading process between grades 2-8. The standardisation was on 15000 pupils from various school systems and states. Norms, reliabilities and equivalence of forms are all satisfactory. The intercorrelations and reliabilities of the sub-tests, essential to profile interpretation, are presented clearly. Validity data is also adequate.

The manual is extremely helpful. The suggestions for interpreting the results and planning a suitable remedial programme are well considered and clearly presented. This test is a most impressive one.

TRN	Name of test	Author	Country	Publisher	Year
89	*Woodcock Reading Mastery Tests*	R. W. Woodcock	USA	American Guidance Service, Inc. (NFER and Educational Evaluation Enterprises act as agents)	1973

Type	No. of forms	C.A. range	Skills tested	Time
Individual, diagnostic	2 (A & B)	5 : 0 to 18 : 0	1. Letter recognition	20'-30'
			2. Word recognition	
			3. Word attack	
			4. Word comprehension	
			5. Passage comprehension	
(level A)			6. Total reading power (combination of 1-5)	

Comments: These five tests provide continuous scales of measurement from kindergarten to the eighteen-year-old level. Thus the tests are geared to a hierarchy of attainments which can be considered as a criterion-referenced scale of reading abilities. The initial interpretation of the results is on the instructional implications for the child, rather than to compare him with his peers. For teachers wishing to consider inter-individual differences, raw scores can also be converted to traditional normative scores. The use of the test as a diagnostic instrument is based on the interpretation of the child's performance profile on the five tests and through the use of a criterion-referenced scale. The interpretation of a pupil's mastery score in any area of the test can readily be related to Informal Reading Inventory standards. This is a consequence of a novel method of item analysis that has been used.

The test has been under development since 1966, and is based on an extensive programme of research. The normative data is based on 3000 subjects specially selected to represent grades K to 12 (five to eighteen-year-olds) throughout the USA. The test appears acceptably reliable.

This test is an interesting development, though whether a criterion-referenced test and a normative one, *of value to the reading teacher*, can be based on the same material raises many complex technical issues of test construction and validation. The manual is most impressive, combining clarity and brevity. Currently the British Intelligence Scale Unit under the direction of Dr C. D. Elliott of the University of Manchester is developing a number of ability scales, including one of reading based on techniques used by Woodcock.

TRN	Name of test	Author	Country	Publisher	Year
90	*Word Clues Test*	S. E. Taylor, H. Frackenpohl and A. S. McDonald	USA	Educational Development Laboratories	1965

Type	No. of forms	C.A. range	Skills tested	Time
Group or individual mastery test (level A)	2 (A & B)	13 : 0 to 18 : 0+	Extent to which context can be used to determine word meaning	Untimed (40'-45')

Comments: This ninety-eight-item test contains fourteen words for each of seven years. The interpretation of the test results is related to a series of books intended to provide materials that will help the students develop their vocabularies. The test is a mastery test, and not primarily concerned with inter-individual differences. (A second version is available for the student who wishes to carry out his own assessment.) The handbook contains no information on standardisations, reliabilities or validities. On the face of it one suspects a mastery test with as few as fourteen items per year of age, but many popular tests have far fewer.

This test is commented on as it is an example of a mastery or content criterion-referenced test related to a specific series of instructional books. It may well be that normative test statistics are not pertinent to the description of the characteristics of such tests, though other mastery test constructors have made greater efforts to cope with the technical aspects of mastery test construction.

4 Attitude to reading scales

(a) *British*

TRN	Name of test	Author	Country	Publisher	Year
19	*Dunham Attitude to Reading Scale*	J. Dunham	B	Unpublished dissertation*	1956

Type	No. of forms	C.A. range	Skills tested	Time
Group, attitude (Thurstone-Chave scale) (level A)	1	Juniors	Attitude to reading	Untimed (15′)

Comments: This is a twenty-item scale covering the entire range of children's attitudes towards reading. The children with whom it is used usually know what is being assessed and therefore might give incorrect responses to please the tester or teacher. The scale is acceptably reliable and valid according to Dunham (re-test reliability 0·77; correlation of scale with teachers' ratings 0·59).

Whether it is legitimate to consider 'attitude to reading' to be a unidimensional trait, is open to question.

* University of Birmingham, Department of Education, 'Attitude and Achievement in Reading'.

TRN	Name of test	Author	Country	Publisher	Year
33	*Georgiades' Attitude to Reading Scale*	N. Georgiades	B	Article by Georgiades in Downing, J. and Brown, A. L. (1967), *The Second International Reading Symposium*, London: Cassell.	1967

Type	No. of forms	C.A. range	Skills tested	Time
Group, oral administration (Likert-type scale)	1	Primary school	Attitude to reading	Untimed (25′)
(level A)				

Comments: This attitude scale contains twenty-two items of which only seven are related to reading. Thus the children are unaware of the specific focus of the scale. This scale is enjoyed greatly by children because of the novelty of its presentation. Georgiades gives few details of standardisation or reliabilities. Despite this, the test technique has considerable potential for development.

TRN	Name of test	Author	Country	Publisher	Year
88	*Williams' Reading Attitude Scale*	G. Williams	B	Unpublished dissertation*	1965

Type	No. of forms	C.A. range	Skills tested	Time
Group or individual, oral administration (Thurstone-Chave model)	1	8 : 6 to 9 : 6	Attitude to reading (25 items)	Untimed (25′)
(level A)				

Comments: This scale comprises twenty-five statements ranging from a highly unfavourable to a highly favourable attitude towards reading. The scale was constructed on the basis of statements contributed by teachers of reading. It was tested for reliabilities and validities with groups of nine-year-old children. The use of the scale involves considerable preparation and is best used with small groups of children. Its major weakness is its 'visibility'—it is fairly clear what the tester is getting at and this might cause some children to present the response they feel is required rather than their real attitudes to reading. It seems likely that the test could be used with other ages, but this requires further investigation.

* University of Manchester, Department of Education, dissertation for the Diploma in the Education of Handicapped Children: 'A study of reading attitude among nine-year-old children'.

(b) *Others*

TRN	Name of test	Author	Country	Publisher	Year
32	*Generalised Attitude Scales*	H. H. Remmers	USA	Best source is Shaw, M. E. and Wright, J. M. (1967) *Scales for the Measurement of Attitudes*, New York: McGraw-Hill	1960

Type (All group or individual)	No. of forms	C.A. range	Skills tested	Time Untimed
Thurstone-type scale	2 (A & B)	18 : 0+	Attitude towards any practice	(10′)
Thurstone-type scale	2 (A & B)	18 : 0+	Attitude towards any occupation	(10′)
Thurstone-type scale	2 (A & B)	15 : 0+	Attitude towards any school subject	(10′)

(level A)

Comments: Generalised attitude scales have been shown to have acceptable reliabilities and validities, but they are still rather crude psychometric instruments. The above group are referred to because each can be adapted to a variety of aspects of reading as a skill, an occupation or a subject. The book by Shaw and Wright discusses the strengths and weaknesses of such scales.

TRN	Name of test	Author	Country	Publisher	Year
71	*Reader's Inventory*	G. D. Spache and S. E. Taylor	USA	Educational Developmental Laboratories	1963

Type	No. of forms	C.A. range	Skills tested	Time
Group or individual, diagnostic	1	11 : 0 to adult	(This is a *checklist* rather than a test) I. (1) Comprehension and study reading habits (2) Rate and flexibility (3) Vocabulary (4) Attitudes and interests II. Visual survey III. Background of experience IV. Expectations from the course	Untimed
(level A)				

Comments: The purpose of this eighty-three item inventory is to enable reading teachers and their students to obtain some insight into the students' study habits, skills, attitudes and interests in relation to reading. The questions concerning each of the aspects listed above are scattered, rather than arranged in groups, in the student's booklet. Interpretations of responses are suggested. The inventory can be used as a basis for discussing a student's reading problems. It is suggested that the results of other testing can be combined with the inventory results and used to plan a programme of activities likely to improve the student's reading skills, study habits, interests and attitudes. No data on standardisation, reliability or validity are presented. Despite this considerable weakness—surprising from so eminent an authority on reading and testing as Dr Spache—the inventory appears to have considerable promise particularly in the individual counselling situation.

TRN	Name of test	Author	Country	Publisher	Year
77	*Science Research Associates Reading Checklist*	V. S. Larsen, P. L. Mastropier, J. A. Harris and G. E. Wainwright	USA	Science Research Associates	1966

Type	No. of forms	C.A. range	Skills tested	Time
Individual questionnaire completed by teacher in respect of pupil	1	Primary school	I. *Preparation for reading:* A. Physical factors B. Cognitive, intellectual and linguistic factors C. Social, personality and environmental factors II. *Values in reading:* A. Depth of interest B. Motives for reading III. *Mechanics of reading:* A. Individual words B. Comprehension of words and short passages C. Comprehension of longer passages	Untimed
(level A)				

Comments: A checklist is not a standardised test. It is designed as a supplement to such tests by summarising the teachers' evaluation of a child's observed reading behaviours. It can also be used to indicate change in the teacher's perception of a child's reading behaviours by administering it twice during a course of instruction in reading.

This particular checklist is linked via the handbook to a series of *Reading Checklist Exercises*. On the whole, it is a rather elementary instrument with an emphasis on mechanical aspects of reading.

The complexity of attitudes to reading

Children's attitudes towards reading may be more complex than some of the preceding scales might suggest. The uses of Osgood's (Osgood *et al.* 1957) semantic differential and Kelly's (1955) repertory grid techniques in attitude measurement have met with some success. Certainly these techniques assume that attitudes are multi- rather than uni-dimensional. Both techniques have been used to measure children's attitudes towards reading in this country.

References

KELLY, G. A. (1955) *Psychology of Personal Constructs* New York: Norton.

OSGOOD, C. E., SUCI, G. J. and TANNENBAUM, P. H. (1957) *The Measurement of Meaning* Urbana: University of Illinois Press.

Blank test summary sheets

TRN	Name of test	Author	Country	Publisher	Year

Type	No. of forms	C.A. range	Skills tested	Time

Comments:

TRN	Name of test	Author		Country	Publisher		Year

Type		No. of forms	C.A. range	Skills tested			Time

Comments:

TRN	Name of test	Author	Country	Publisher	Year

Type		No. of forms	C.A. range	Skills tested	Time

Comments:

TRN	Name of test	Author	Country	Publisher	Year

Type	No. of forms	C.A. range	Skills tested	Time

Comments:

TRN	Name of test	Author	Country	Publisher	Year

Type	No. of forms	C.A. range	Skills tested	Time

Comments:

TRN	Name of test	Author	Country	Publisher	Year

Type		No. of forms	C.A. range	Skills tested	Type

Comments:

Appendix 1

Publishers and distributors of reading tests and test information

British

Basil Blackwell, Broad Street, Oxford, Oxfordshire.

*British American Optical, Radlett Road, Watford, Herts.

Cassell and Co. Limited, 35 Red Lion Square, London WC1.

*Cassell Collier and Macmillan Publishers Limited, Blue Star House, Highgate Hill, London N19 5NY.

Centre for the Teaching of Reading, 29 Eastern Avenue, Reading, Berkshire RG1 5RU.

Chatto and Windus Limited, 42 William IV Street, London WC2.

Crosby and Lockwood and Son Limited, 26 Old Brompton Road, London SW7.

Educational Evaluation Enterprises, 5 Marsh Street, Bristol BS1 4AE.

Gibson (Robert) and Son Limited, 2 West Regent Street, Glasgow C2.

Ginn and Company Limited (Test Services), 18 Bedford Row, London WC1R 4EJ.

Godfrey Thomson Unit for Academic Assessment, The University of Edinburgh, 24 Buccleuch Place, Edinburgh EH8 9JT.

Harrap and Company Limited, 182 High Holborn, London WC1.

Heinemann Educational Limited, 48 Charles Street, London W1X 8AH.

Hodder and Stoughton Educational, St Paul's House, Warwick Lane, London EC4P 4AH.

H. K. Lewis and Company Limited, 136 Gower Street, London WC1E 6BS.

*McGraw-Hill Book Co., Shoppenhangers Road, Maidenhead, Berkshire.

Macmillan and Company Limited, Little Essex Street, London WC2.

National Foundation for Educational Research in England and Wales Test Agency, 2 Jennings Buildings, Thames Avenue, Windsor, Berkshire SL4 1QS.

Thomas Nelson and Sons Limited, Lincoln Way, Windmill Road, Sunbury-on-Thames, Middlesex TW16 7HP; *or* 36 Park Street, London W1Y 4DE.

Newnes Limited, Tower House, Southampton Street, London WC2.

Oliver and Boyd, 39 Welbeck Street, London W1.

Oxford University Press, Ely House, 37 Dover Street, London W1X 4AH.

Psychological Test Publications, Scamps Court, Pilton Street, Barnstaple, Devon.

Royal National Institute for the Deaf, 105 Gower Street, London WC1.

*Science Research Associates Limited, Reading Road, Henley-on-Thames, Oxfordshire RG9 1EW.

* English branches of American companies.

K

*Scott Foresman and Company, 32 West Street, Brighton, Sussex BN1 2RT.

Staples Press Limited, Cavendish Place, London W1.

University of Aston in Birmingham, Gosta Green, Birmingham B4 7ET.

University of London Press Limited, see Hodder and Stoughton Educational.

West Sussex Local Educational Authority, Education Department, County Hall, Chichester, Sussex.

Further useful information on the assessment of reading (*British*)

The following organisations produce materials related to the testing and assessment of reading abilities as part of a more general concern with the facilitation of children's learning.

United Kingdom Reading Association (UKRA), S. Heatlie, Esq., Hon. Gen. Sec., 63 Laurel Grove, Sunderland SR2 9EE.

The association publishes a journal, *Reading*, three times yearly. The reports of annual conferences are published regularly. A series of monographs on topics related to reading is also available and a variety of smaller publications. UKRA also act as distributors for materials published by the International Reading Association.

National Association for Remedial Education (NARE), R. Cooper, Esq., 77 Chignall Road, Chelmsford, Essex CM1 2JA.

This association publishes a journal *Remedial Education*, three times yearly. It is also moving into the field of publishing in its

own right, as the books by Atkinson and Gains (1973) and McNicholas and McEntee (1973) described in Appendix 2 indicate.

The Centre for the Teaching of Reading, University of Reading School of Education, 29 Eastern Avenue, Reading RG1 5RU.

The Remedial Supply Co., Dixon Street, Wolverhampton, Staffordshire.

The above company provides a catalogue of remedial materials and apparatus with particular emphasis on reading.

The National Book League, 7 Albemarle Street, London W1.

Their travelling exhibition *Help in Reading* includes books for teachers on the assessment and diagnosis of reading disabilities plus a large amount of reading material suitable for children of all ages who are backward in reading.

The Reading Centre, Alastair Hendry, Esq., Lecturer in Primary Education, Craigie College of Education, Ayr, Scotland.

The above centre is given as *an example* of the centres being set up at many Colleges of Education throughout England, Wales and Scotland. At such centres one is likely to be able to discuss the contribution of the assessment of reading abilities and attitudes to the improvement of standards of literacy. The very considerable national and local sources of such information are considered in detail in a forthcoming publication (Pumfrey, in press).

American and other English-speaking companies

American Guidance Service, 720 Washington Avenue S.E., Minneapolis 14, Minnesota, USA.

Australian Council for Educational Research, Test and Allied Services Department, Frederick Street, Hawthorn E2, Victoria, Australia.

Better Reading Program Incorporated, 230 East Ohio Street, Chicago 11, Illinois, USA.

Bobbs-Merrill Company Incorporated, 4300 West 62nd Street, Indianapolis 6, Indiana, USA.

Bureau of Educational Measurements, Kansas State Teachers College, Emporia, Kansas 66801, USA.

Bureau of Publications, Teachers College, Columbia University, 525 West 120 Street, New York 27, New York, USA.

California Test Bureau, 5916 Hollywood Boulevard, Los Angeles, California 90028, USA.

Committee on Diagnostic Reading Tests Incorporated, Mountain Home, North Carolina 28758, North Carolina, USA.

Consulting Psychologists Press, 577 College Avenue, Palo Alto, California, USA.

Cooperative Test Division, Educational Testing Service, 20 Nassau Street, Princeton, New Jersey, USA.

CTB/McGraw-Hill, Del Monte Research Park, Monterey, California 93940, USA.

Department of Psychological Testing, De Paul University, 25 East Jackson Boulevard, Chicago, Illinois 60604, USA.

Developmental Reading Distributors, 1944 Sheridan Avenue, Laramie, Wyoming 82070, USA.

Educational Development Laboratories, Huntington, New York 11746, New York, USA.

Educational Publishing Company, Darien, Connecticut, USA.

Educational Test Bureau, 720 Washington Avenue S.E., Minneapolis 14, Minnesota 55414, USA.

Follett Publishing Company, 1010 West Washington Boulevard, Chicago 7, Illinois 61822, USA.

Garrard Press, 119 West Park Avenue, Champaign, Illinois 61820, USA.

General Educational Development Testing Service of the American Council on Education, 1785 Massachusetts Avenue N.W., Washington D.C. 20036, USA.

Ginn and Company, 72 Fifth Avenue, New York 10011, New York, USA.

Guidance Testing Associates, 6516 Shirley Avenue, Austin 5, Texas, USA.

Harcourt, Brace and World, 757 Third Avenue, New York 17, New York, USA.

Holt, Rinehart and Winston Incorporated, 383 Madison Avenue, New York, USA.

Houghton Mifflin Company, 432 Park Avenue South, New York, USA; *or* 2 Park Street, Boston 7, Massachusetts, USA.

Institute of Personality and Ability Testing, 1608 Coronada Drive, Champaign, Illinois, USA.

Language Research Associates, 300 North State Street, Chicago 60610, Illinois, USA.

J. B. Lippincott and Company, East Washington Square, Philadelphia, Pennsylvania 19106, USA.

Longman, Browne and Nolan, 4 Southgrape Georges Street, Dublin 2, Eire.

Macmillan Company, Front and Brown Streets, Riverside, New Jersey 08075, USA.

New Zealand Council for Educational Research, Education House, 178 Willis Street, Wellington C2, New Zealand.

Ohio State University, University Publications Sales, 242 West 18th Avenue, Columbus, Ohio 43210, USA.

Ohio Testing Services, State Department of Education, 751 Northwest Boulevard, Columbus, Ohio 43212, USA.

Ontario College of Education, Guidance Centre, University of Toronto, 371 Bloor Street West, Toronto 5, Ontario, Canada.

Personnel Press Incorporated, 191 Spring Street, Lexington, Massachusetts 02173, USA.

Prentice-Hall Incorporated, Englewood Cliffs, New Jersey 07632, USA.

Psychological Corporation, 304 East 45th Street, New York 10017, USA (NFER are British agents for the above).

Psychological Institute, P.O. Box 1118, Lake Alfred, Florida, USA.

Psychometric Affiliates, Chicago Plaza, Brookport, Illinois 62910, USA.

Scholastic Testing Service Incorporated, 3774 West Devon Avenue, Chicago 45, Illinois, USA.

Science Research Associates Incorporated, 259 East Erie Street, Chicago 11, Illinois 60611, USA.

Scott Foresman and Company, 433 East Erie Street, Chicago, Illinois 60611, USA.

Sheridan Psychological Services Incorporated, P.O. Box 837, Beverley Hills, California 90213, USA.

C. H. Stoelting Company, 1350 South Kostner Avenue, Chicago, Illinois 60623, USA.

Taylor Center for Controlled Reading and Research, 75 Prospect Street, Huntington, New York 11744, USA.

United States Department of Health, Education and Welfare, U.S. Government Printing Office, Washington D.C. 20402, USA.

University of Illinois Press, Urbana 3, Illinois 61801, USA.

University of Minnesota Press, Minneapolis 14, Minnesota, USA.

Webster Division, McGraw-Hill Book Company, 1154 Roco Avenue, St Louis, Missouri 63126, USA.

Western Psychological Services, 12031 Wilshire Boulevard, Los Angeles, California, USA.

Further useful sources of information on the assessment of reading (American)

Though their concern is with reading in general, each of the following organisations has available a great deal of information on the testing of reading:

International Reading Association, Six Tyre Avenue, Newark, Delaware 19711, USA.

Educational Resources Information Centre (ERIC) *on Reading and Communication Skills*, 508 South Sixth Street, Champaign, Illinois 61820, USA.

For information concerning tests in general

Educational Resources Information Centre (ERIC) *on Tests, Measurement and Evaluation*, Educational Testing Service, Princeton, New Jersey 08540, USA.

Appendix 2

Annotated book list

One of the reading teacher's major aims is to facilitate children's progress in reading. Assessment techniques and tests describe the child's current level of performance in given areas. They give indications of relative strengths and weaknesses and suggest profitable lines of action for teacher and child. Usually some activity for the child is then engineered by the teacher so as to help the child master a particular skill, thereby enabling the pupil to progress.

The following book list is not intended to be exhaustive. It contains references likely to be of value to the teacher of reading interested in materials and methods that might profitably be applied after an assessment of a child's reading competencies has been carried out. Each book is prefaced by the figures 1 and/or 2.

1 indicates content concerned partly with reading tests and assessment procedures of interest to the teacher wishing to become more knowledgeable in this area.

2 indicates content primarily in terms of activities that can be adapted to a child's assessed reading needs.

If both figures are given, the figure given first indicates the more dominant of the two components.

(2) ABLEWHITE, R. C. (1967) *The Slow Reader* London: Heinemann Educational.

The importance of motivation in improving the reading competencies of slow learning secondary school children is interestingly presented, albeit only from one school. The suggestions for remedial activities will appeal to many teachers—and their pupils.

(2) ATKINSON, E. J. and GAINS, C. W. (1973) *An A-Z List of Reading and Subject Books* Wolverhampton: National Association for Remedial Education.

A most useful compendium of information on the reading ages and interest levels of both graded readers and a wide variety of subject books and materials for primary and secondary school children. Some helpful suggestions concerning the recording of reading progress are made. There is a section on books for adult illiterates. This publication is likely to be particularly helpful to teachers wanting to locate reading materials of parallel difficulty levels.

(1, 2) BOND, G. L. and TINKER, M. A. (1967) *Reading Difficulties, their Diagnosis and Correction* New York: Appleton-Century-Crofts, second edition.

Despite its American origins, this is a valuable source book. The discussion of the nature and causes of reading difficulties leads into their diagnosis and remedial treatment. After considering the principles of remedial instruction, a host of practical suggestions for dealing with particular difficulties is presented.

(2) BRENNAN, W., JACKSON, J. and REEVE, J. (1972) *Look: Visual Perception Materials* London: Macmillan Educational.

The teachers' manual is accompanied by four workbooks. The former outlines the case for specific training in the development of visual perception skills and gives detailed teaching suggestions. The workbooks provide ninety-six 'closely structured exercises' intended to form part of a pre-reading programme. There are a few printing errors and distortions of illustrations which will, presumably, be corrected.

(1, 2) CLARK, M. M. and MILNE, A. (Eds.) (1973) *Reading and Related Skills* London: Ward Lock Educational.

Papers from the 1972 UKRA Conference with major sections devoted to the development of reading skills and training the teachers of reading.

(1, 2) COHEN, S. A. (1969) *Teach Them All To Read* New York: Random House.

This book is concerned with the theory, methods and materials for teaching disadvantaged pupils. It deals with the diagnosis of patterns of failure, the use of tests and records, and lists the sub-skills of reading at each year level. Equally important, are the teaching suggestions.

(1, 2) DANIELS, J. C. and DIACK, H. (1970) *The Standard Reading Tests* London: Chatto and Windus, seventh impression.

A very useful handbook of tests ranging from pre-reading to the fourteen-year-old level. For details see page 103.

(1, 2) DECHANT, E. (Ed.) (1971) *Detection and Correction of Reading Difficulties* New York: Appleton-Century-Crofts.

This is a book of readings covering the nature of reading difficulties, their identification and treatment. Diagnostic testing in particular is given excellent coverage. There is a very helpful section on the uses of the Informal Reading Inventory. Emphasis is given to the remedial teaching of reading at all levels.

(1, 2) DELLA-PIANA, G. M. (1968) *Reading Diagnosis and Prescription* New York: Holt, Rinehart and Winston.

Includes examples of a diagnostic procedure identifying reading difficulties, together with suggestions for treatment. Contains an extensive list of Skill Development Materials.

(2) DUFFY, G. G. and SHERMAN, G. B. (1972) *Systematic Reading Instruction* New York: Harper and Row

The authors focus on specific sequentially arranged reading skills. The skills are described in terms of pupil performances, and examples are given. Objectives of reading instruction, resources and assessment in relation to each sub-skill are considered. A large number of very helpful activities are described.

(1, 2) FRANKLIN, A. W. and NAIDOO, S. (1970) *Assessment and Teaching of Dyslexic Children* London: Invalid Children's Aid Association.

Irrespective of whether one agrees with the value of the concept of dyslexia, this book contains a wealth of practical suggestions for helping children with severe reading difficulties.

(1, 2) GARDNER, K. (Ed.) (1970) *Reading Skills: Theory and Practice* London: Ward Lock Educational.

Papers from the 1969 UKRA Conference including analyses of the sub-skills of reading.

(2) GLYNN, D. M. (1972) *Dominoes* Edinburgh: Oliver and Boyd.

This graded material, using colour photographs, helps provide a link between the child's experiences and the printed word. It is useful ancillary material for children using a language-experience approach to reading. There is no systematic vocabulary control. The teacher's guide gives much sound advice on helping children discover grapheme-phoneme similarities and differences using the materials.

(2) GOODACRE, E. (1969) *A List of Published Reading Schemes for the Primary School* (Obtainable from the author, 24 Brookside Crescent, Cuffley, Potters Bar, Herts.)

Standard information concerning author, publisher, date of publication, approach used, Reading Age range and Interest Age range is provided for each of thirty seven reading schemes.

(1, 2) GOODACRE, E. J. (1972) *Hearing Children Read: Including a List of Reading Schemes and Other Materials* Centre for the Teaching of Reading, University of Reading School of Education.

Goodacre describes ways in which the teacher can organise her observation of children's oral reading so as to provide a basis for devising remedial and facilitative activities for the child. A useful discussion of the types and importance of reading errors made by children is included. The importance of a child's spontaneous re-reading after recognising an oral reading error is emphasised. The role of the tape-recorder in providing the child with an opportunity of recognising such errors is discussed along with other methods of recording errors and miscues.

(1, 2) GUSZAK, F. J. (1972) *Diagnostic Reading Instruction in the Elementary School* New York: Harper and Row.

A systematic approach to the diagnosis and treatment of the reading skill needs of primary school children is presented. The specific objectives of a reading programme are spelled out and activities, likely to facilitate their attainment, described.

(1, 2) HARRIS, A. J. (1970) *How to Increase Reading Ability: a Guide to Developmental and Remedial Methods* New York: David McKay, fifth edition.

The evaluation and diagnosis of individual and group instructional needs is analysed. The final third of the book presents suggestions for the developmental and remedial teaching of specific skills. A useful analysis of the reading sub-skills at various stages of reading development is given.

(2) HUGHES, J. M. (1973) *Aids to Reading* London: Evans, third reprint.

This book gives details of games and activities, programmed materials and machines of use in facilitating children's reading development.

(2) HUGHES, J. M. (1973) *Reading with Phonics* London: Evans.

This is a compendium of activities intended to develop the child's ability to understand phonics. The appropriate treatments for some common reading difficulties are prescribed.

(1) JACKSON, S. (1972) *A Teacher's Guide to Tests and Testing* London: Longmans, third edition.

An excellent introduction to the uses and availability of tests in education. Two chapters are devoted to reading tests.

(1, 2) JACKSON, S. (1972) *Get Reading Right* Glasgow: Gibson.

The manual describes eleven Phonic Skills Tests of a criterion-referenced nature. Helpful ideas on the remediation of weaknesses are described, especially for directional training and the correction of reversals. The accompanying Record Sheets provide a valuable summary of children's progress.

(2) KELLY, T. A. (Ed.) (1973) *Teacher's Guide to Reading Schemes for Slow Learners* Sandwell LEA Child Psychology Service, Child Guidance Centre, West Bromwich.

The aim of this useful handbook is to help teachers select reading materials suited to the needs of individual children. Kelly presents information concerning the structure, appeal and content of a number of comprehensive reading schemes with particular reference to their value in remedial situations. Reading Ages and Interest Ages of the series and of supplementary readers are also given. The focus is on books that have been found helpful in the early and middle stages of learning to read. Thus the majority of the material described has reading ages up to about the ten-year-old level. A way of using the guide to match the distribution of books in a school class to the pattern of reading abilities of the pupils is described. Teachers using this system will generally become more efficient in meeting the reading requirements of their pupils.

(1, 2) KIRK, S. A. and KIRK, W. D. (1972) *Psycholinguistic Learning Disabilities: Diagnosis and Remediation* Urbana: University of Illinois Press.

This book contains an exposition of the rationale of the Illinois Test of Psycholinguistic Abilities. Relationships between ITPA sub-test scores and certain reading disabilities are reported. Patterns of disability in psycholinguistic profiles and their interpretation are discussed. The last two chapters offer guidelines for the remediation of psycholinguistic disabilities in specific functions.

(1, 2) LABON, D. (1972) *Assessment of Reading Ability* (and associated booklets) Chichester: West Sussex LEA.

This is one of a series of publications giving advice on the assessment and treatment of reading difficulties at the primary school level.

(2) LAWSON, K. S. (1968) *Children's Reading* University of Leeds Institute of Education, Paper No. 8.

Six lists of books are presented. The first four describe Reading Series and Graded Reading Schemes for primary and secondary school age pupils respectively. These are followed by two lists, each having nine sections, of School Subject Series suitable for primary and secondary school children. The information given is minimal, comprising usually of the number in the series, Reading Age, Interest Age and publisher. Despite the absence of critical comments, the booklet provides a useful overview of the materials available at the time.

(2, 1) MCCREESH, J. and MAHER, A. (1974) *Remedial Education Objectives and Techniques* London: Ward Lock Educational.

The authors apply principles of curriculum development to the analysis of reading failure and the planning of remedial activities. An analysis of the nature and role of perception in relation to the learning process is presented. This leads to a discussion of techniques for the diagnosis of perceptual difficulties, followed by the specification of objectives of the remedial teaching of reading. The authors then describe various techniques that they consider appropriate to alleviating particular types of auditory, visual and psychomotor difficulties that may adversely affect children's ability to read. The contribution of educational technology to the remedial teaching of reading is considered and specific materials described. The importance of the evaluation and assessment of the effects of remedial work is briefly considered.

(2) MCNICHOLAS, J. and MCENTEE, J. (1973) *Games to Develop Reading Skills* Wolverhampton: National Association for Remedial Education.

A description of games that can be used to develop particular reading skills in the classroom is given. The links between reading games and the skills that they are intended to develop are often more complicated than appears to be the case at first sight. The authors are aware of this and also of the dangers implicit in the competitive aspects of games. The ideas presented are generally appropriate to primary school children but could be adapted for use with older groups. The games described can be made from inexpensive material. A helpful reading list indicating other sources of reading games is given.

(1, 2) MELNIK, A. and MERRITT, J. (Eds.) (1972) *The Reading Curriculum* London: Hodder and Stoughton Educational in association with the Open University Press.

This book is included in the Open University multi-media course on reading development. It contains analyses of reading skills in various content areas, a discussion of the development of reading competence, the theory and practice of the diagnostic teaching of reading and a section on the assessment of reading. This very reasonably priced book brings together a host of contributions worthy of the consideration of any teacher interested in reading.

(1, 2) MILES, T. R. (1970) *On Helping the Dyslexic Child* London: Methuen.

Miles describes the difficulties in reading faced by dyslexic children. He gives suggestions concerning the conduct of remedial work with different types of dyslexia. Considerable emphasis is given to the importance of using rules in spelling. The book ends with a specimen dictionary and spelling exercises.

(2, 1) MOSELEY, D. (1975) *Special Provision for Readers*: *When will they ever learn?* Windsor: NFER Publishing Company.

After an extensive review of provision for helping children with reading difficulties, Moseley concludes that the wider implementation of approaches already tried and found effective would greatly reduce the incidence of reading failure in our schools. The book outlines a variety of promising practices whilst, equally valuably, pointing to weaknesses that could be rectified. Whilst claiming that considerable progress has been made in the remedial teaching of reading both within particular schools and by certain LEA remedial education services, much remains to be done. Inner-city schools and secondary schools are two situations where the needs of children with reading difficulties are frequently not met. The book documents many interesting innovations.

(2, 1) MOYLE, D. (1968) *The Teaching of Reading* London: Ward Lock Educational.

Provides many practical suggestions concerning the organisation of the teaching of reading in school. Suggested exercises for children based on a logical progression are likely to be of value to many teachers.

(2) MOYLE, D. and MOYLE, L. (1972) *Modern Innovations in the Teaching of Reading* London: Hodder and Stoughton Educational.

Contains succinct descriptions of a wide variety of recently produced methods and materials that can be adapted to the different reading needs of both children making normal progress and those finding particular difficulties. Whilst predominantly concerned with early and intermediate reading competencies, some of the items described are suitable for older age groups.

(1, 2) National Book League (1972) *Help in Reading: Books for the Teacher of Backward Children and for Pupils Backward in Reading* London: National Book League.

This is the annotated catalogue of a specially selected NBL exhibition. The teaching of reading, diagnosis of disabilities and remediation are represented therein by eminent authorities. Books for children are graded by reading and interest ages.

(2, 1) PAULL, M. E. and HASKELL, S. H. (1972) *Training in Basic Cognitive Skills* Harlow: Educational Supply Association.

The twenty eight children's booklets aim at providing a training programme of pre-reading exercises for children aged between two and six years, and for older handicapped children in some cases. The kit makes available materials likely to facilitate the development of a variety of discriminations and coordinations predominantly related to the visual, motor and language areas. The exercises can be used for prescriptive remedial work.

(1) PUMFREY, P. D. (In preparation) *Measuring Reading Abilities. Concepts, Sources and Applications* London: Hodder and Stoughton Educational.

Intended for the non-mathematician, the book considers the role of measurement and assessment in the monitoring and improvement of reading attainments and attitudes.

(1, 2) REID, J. F. (Ed.) (1972) *Reading: Problems and Practices* London: Ward Lock Educational.

This is a selection of papers covering theoretical aspects, research findings, and practical considerations of the assessment, diagnosis and treatment of reading difficulties.

(2) RICHARDSON, J. A. and HART, J. A. (1967) *Books for the Retarded Reader* Victoria: Australian Council for Educational Research, third edition.

Information on length, Reading Age, Interest Age, covers, printing, illustrations and vocabulary of a wide range of schemes, supplementary readers and school library books is presented. The authors give a critical appraisal of the series described. Books have been classified under nine headings.

The first two of these outline series and supplementary reading materials that have been specifically written for teaching the skills underlying reading to older backward readers.

(2) RUSSELL, D. H. and KARP, E. (1961) *Reading Aids through the Grades. Three Hundred Developmental Reading Activities* New York: Bureau of Publications, Teachers College, Columbia University, ninth printing.

The activities listed stress the developmental importance of various reading related activities. The teacher can find suggestions for helping pupils of any age from kindergarten to tertiary education.

(2) RUSSELL, D. H. and RUSSELL, E. R. (1965) *Listening Aids through the Grades. One Hundred and Ninety Listening Activities* New York: Bureau of Publications, Teacher's College, Columbia University, sixth printing.

A very popular and useful handbook of suggestions for improving children's listening skills.

(1, 2) SAMPSON, O. C. (1975) *Remedial Education* London; Routledge and Kegan Paul.

From a pioneer educational psychologist and researcher in the field of the remedial teaching of reading comes a valuable overview of the development and current position of remedial education in Britain. The effects of the remedial teaching of reading are critically examined, as are the skills of the remedial teacher in relation to (i) testing and recording and (ii) selection of methods and materials. The complexity of the remedial teaching of reading is lucidly discussed, some important current conceptual and practical problems are considered and constructive suggestions made for resolving these.

(1, 2) SCHELL, L. M. and BURNS, P. C. (Eds.) (1972) *Remedial Reading: Classroom and Clinic* New York: Allyn and Bacon, second edition.

A book of readings concerning theory, research and practical aspects of the remedial teaching of reading.

(1) SCHOFIELD, H. (1972) *Assessment and Testing: an Introduction* London: Unwin Education Books.

The author provides a simple explanation of basic terms in assessment and testing suitable for the non-mathematician. The discussion is extended to test and assessment procedures in the fields of intelligence, abilities, personality and sociometry.

(1, 2) SCHONELL, F. J. and SCHONELL, F. E. (1962) *Diagnostic and Attainment Testing* London: Oliver and Boyd.

This book starts with a discussion of testing in educational practice. The tests contained in the section concerned with reading are described and commented on in Chapter 4, page 100.

(2) STOTT, D. H. (1971) *Programmed Reading Kit* Edinburgh: Holmes McDougall, second edition.

The kit comprises a series of thirty graded, largely self-correcting, card games. These are claimed to enable a complete non-reader to achieve a reading age of nine years on completion of the series. The material has been found of considerable value in both the normal classroom and in the remedial teaching situation.

(2) STOTT, D. H. (1972) *Flying Start—Learning-to-Learn Kit* Edinburgh: Holmes McDougall.

This kit of materials consists of individual and group games which are mainly self-corrective. The materials are claimed to be a systematic programme at the pre-reading level, of activities in which good learning strategies are reinforced in situations which allow the child opportunities for initiative and choice. It leads into Stott's *Programmed Reading Kit*.

(1, 2) STRANG, R. (1969) *Diagnostic Teaching of Reading* New York: McGraw-Hill, second edition.

Achieves a balance between identifying and teaching isolated skills whilst accepting the essential integration of the child's reading behaviours. Testing, observation and record keeping are well discussed. A plan for diagnosis and remediation based on improving a child's skills in his areas of greatest weakness is presented.

(1, 2) TANSLEY, A. E. (1972) *Reading and Remedial Reading* London: Routledge and Kegan Paul.

This is the paperback edition of a 1967 publication. It aims at a diagnostic approach towards the assessment and treatment of reading difficulties. The first half of the book is concerned with assessing and facilitating reading readiness. The second is more directed towards remedial programmes. Both sections emphasise the importance of neurological development. The book contains many practical suggestions for improving motor and perceptual skills and coordinations.

(2, 1) WALLEN, C. J. (1972) *Competency in Teaching Reading*. (2, 1) HARP, W. and WALLEN, C. J. (1972) *Instructor's Guide to 'Competency in Teaching Reading' and 'The First R: Readings on Teaching Reading'*. (1) SEBESTA, S. L. and WALLEN, C. J. (1972) *The First R: Readings on the Teaching of Reading* All Henley-on-Thames: Science Research Associates.

The above three books were developed for a reading methods course. 'The first R' provides the reader with an understanding of the psychological and cultural context in which reading instruction occurs. The other book and its instructor's manual focus on translating principles into practice. Over two-thirds of the text is devoted to application. The emphasis is on the diagnostic teaching of reading in which testing and teaching are complementary. A taxonomy of reading objectives, testing procedures and teaching strategies forms the basis of the book. Whilst much of the content will seem obvious to the experienced teacher of reading, the structure of the book and the mass of concrete suggestions for developing prescribed skills is impressive.

(2) WEBSTER, J. (1965) *Practical Reading* London: Evans.

A collection of various classroom techniques that have been valuable in helping children with severe reading difficulties. The visual-verbal method devised by the author is described. This technique can be adapted to pupils of any age.

(2, 1) WILSON, R. M. (1967) *Diagnostic and Remedial Reading for Classroom and Clinic* Columbus: Merrill.

Wilson presents a lucid discussion of the diagnosis of reading failure. Specific advice on the remediation of orientation difficulties, vocabulary difficulties and comprehension difficulties is given. The parents' role in diagnosis, remediation and prevention of reading failure is considered.

Index

*Reading tests are indexed
separately, by title, on pages 45-7.*